SINGER

SEWING REFERENCE LIBRARY®

Creative Sewing Ideas

Cy DeCosse Incorporated
Minnetonka, Minnesota

SINGER
◆═══ SEWING REFERENCE LIBRARY® ═══◆
Creative Sewing Ideas

Contents

Copyright © 1990
Cy DeCosse Incorporated
5900 Green Oak Drive
Minnetonka, Minnesota 55343
1-800-328-3895
All rights reserved
Printed in U.S.A.

Also available from the publisher: *Sewing Essentials, Sewing for the Home, Clothing Care & Repair, Sewing for Style, Sewing Specialty Fabrics, Sewing Activewear, The Perfect Fit, Timesaving Sewing, More Sewing for the Home, Tailoring, Sewing for Children, Sewing with an Overlock, 101 Sewing Secrets, Sewing Pants That Fit, Quilting by Machine, Decorative Machine Stitching*

Library of Congress
Cataloging-in-Publication Data

Creative sewing ideas.

p.cm. — (Singer sewing reference library)
Includes index.
ISBN 0-86573-258-2
ISBN 0-86573-259-0 (pbk.)
1. Machine sewing. 2. Textile fabrics.
I. Cy DeCosse Incorporated. II. Series.
TT713.C75 1990
646.2'044 — dc20   90-42685

Distributed by: Contemporary Books, Inc.
  Chicago, Illinois

CY DE COSSE INCORPORATED
Chairman: Cy DeCosse
President: James B. Maus
Executive Vice President: William B. Jones

CREATIVE SEWING IDEAS
Created by: The Editors of Cy DeCosse Incorporated, in cooperation with the Sewing Education Department, Singer Sewing Company. Singer is a trademark of The Singer Company and is used under license.

Executive Editor: Zoe A. Graul
Technical Director: Rita C. Opseth
Project Manager: Linda Halls
Senior Art Director: Lisa Rosenthal
Writer: Rita C. Opseth
Editors: Janice Cauley, Bernice Maehren
Sample Coordinator: Carol Olson
Technical Photo Director: Bridget Haugh
Sewing Staff: Phyllis Galbraith, Bridget
Haugh, Linda Neubauer, Carol Olson,
Lori Ritter, Nancy Sundeen
Fabric Editor: Joanne Wawra
Photo Studio Manager: Rebecca DaWald
Photographers: Jana Frieband, Rex Irmen,
John Lauenstein, Bill Lindner, Mark
Macemon, Charles Nields, Mette
Nielsen, Mike Parker, Cathleen Shannon,
Marc Sholtes

Director of Development, Planning &
Production: Jim Bindas
Production Manager: Amelia Merz
Production Art Supervisor: Julie Churchill
Production Staff: Joe Fahey, Kevin D. Frakes,
Melissa Grabanski, Mark Jacobson, Yelena
Konrardy, Daniel Meyers, Linda Schloegel,
Greg Wallace, Nik Wogstad
Consultants: Roberta Carr, Ann Fatigati,
Wendy Fedie, Linda Froiland, Carolyn
Golberg, Pamela Hastings, Janet Hethorn,
David Hill, Kenneth D. King, Janet Klaer,
Marit Kucera, Andrea McCormick,
Katherine McMahon, Herman W. Phynes
III, Suzanne Stout, Marcy Tilton,
Joanne Wawra

Contributors: Burda Patterns Inc.; Butterick
Patterns; C. J. Enterprises; C. M. Offray
& Son, Inc.; Coats & Clark Inc.; Decart
Inc.; Dell Fabrics; Dritz Corporation;
Exotic Silks; Fabrics on the Mall; The
Green Pepper, Inc.; HTC-Handler Textile
Corporation; International Bead & Sequin,
Inc.; KM²; Madeira; The McCall Pattern
Company; Minnesota Fabrics, Inc.; Olfa
Products Corporation; Pellon Division,
Freudenberg Nonwovens; Scandia Down
Shops; Simplicity Pattern Co. Inc.; Spartex
Inc.; Swiss-Metrosene, Inc.; Tandy Leather
Co.; Treadle Yard Goods; © 1989 United
Wallcoverings; Vogue Patterns; YLI
Corporation
Color Separations: Multi-Scan International
Reproduction A/S, Denmark
Printing: Ringier America, Inc. (1190)

Introduction

As a home sewer, you use creativity in every project you sew when selecting patterns, fabrics, and sewing techniques. This natural ability to create can be expanded into new areas. For example, you may want to try your hand at fabric painting or experiment with different ways to accent garment seamlines.

Inspiration is the first step. New ideas can be found everywhere. *Creative Sewing Ideas* will help you create new designs, textures, and color schemes.

The Creating Fabrics section presents a number of techniques for changing the appearance, texture, or design of a fabric for a new effect. Silk fabric can be

twisted for a crinkled appearance, or acid-washed to achieve the look and feel of suede. The texture of wool fabric can be changed by machine washing and drying it, creating a felted wool that is thicker and more compact than the original wool. Designs can be created on rayon, cotton, or linen fabrics by *discharge dyeing,* or removing some of the dye; and most fabrics can be painted or screen printed.

In the Creative Details section, learn several techniques for sewing decorative seams, including those that are edgestitched, fringed, frayed, and bound. Another method for sewing seams uses the selvage to create

the look of a decorative trim. There are also instructions for adding new seams to a pattern.

Double or triple piping can outline and highlight seamlines and edges. And creative pockets, such as window or foldover pockets, can add interest to a garment. Or sew triangular pockets or buttonholes, which are variations of the traditional welt pocket and bound buttonhole.

In the Embellishments section, see how extra touches, such as braids, ribbons, and beads, can make a simple garment more creative. Slentre braid, which can be custom-made to enhance the colors of a garment, is

simple to make. Ribbonwork, used on garments in the past, can embellish current fashions; two ribbonwork designs are included in this section. Beadwork, which has been used to adorn garments for years, is still prominent in evening wear. We have included both machine and hand methods for attaching beads.

The Creative Projects section helps you get started with your creative sewing. Complete instructions for simple zippered bags, portfolios, and belts are given in this section. These basic designs provide an opportunity to use the creative ideas found throughout the book.

Looking for Inspiration

The starting point for creativity is the inspiration, whether you are trying to decide on a design to screen print or determine the shape of a pocket. Inspiration can be found everywhere by looking closely at the colors, shapes, and textures around you. Nature is a good source of inspiration, from the many different tree shapes to the colors of the leaves or buds. Adapt a wallpaper design to make a stencil for screen printing, weave the colors of an iris into a slentre braid trim, or use a kitchen utensil to apply an interesting painted design to fabric.

Historical or ethnic garments can also be inspiring. An interesting pocket shape or a unique belt design from these garments can complement today's fashions.

Inspiration can be found in many objects by looking at the designs, shapes, colors, and textures.

Nature is a good source of inspiration for color. A single flower, for example, may contain many subtle shades.

Wallpaper can inspire a fabric design. The fish and shell designs were enlarged and adapted to make the stencils for screen printing the fabric.

Books can offer a wide selection of design ideas. This geometric design has been adapted for the beadwork on the cuffs of an evening dress.

Creating
Fabrics

Creativity with Fabrics

Fabric offers many opportunities for creativity. You can change the appearance of a fabric by changing the surface design or by changing the structure of the fabric. For example, a plain fabric can be made more interesting by adding a design using discharge dyeing or screen printing, or a wool fabric can be felted to make compact, thick cloth.

Twisted silk is made by tightly twisting lightweight silk fabric while it is wet, then machine drying it to heat-set the crinkled look.

Acid-washed silk is created by machine washing lightweight silk fabric with a solution of vinegar and water. This makes the fabric softer and gives it a sueded or brushed appearance.

Painting on fabric and leather adds colorful designs to the surface.

Wool felting changes the structure of wool fabric by shrinking it considerably. Felting makes the fabric thicker and more compact and changes the surface texture.

Discharge dyeing creates a design on the fabric by using bleach to remove some of the dye.

Screen printing creates a design on the fabric by using inks to add color.

Twisted Silk

The look of China silk or silk broadcloth can be changed by twisting the fabric to give it a unique texture. The fabric is first soaked in lukewarm water and then twisted tightly into a ball. The ball of twisted fabric is machine dried; the textural wrinkling that occurs is heat-set by the dryer.

A garment made from this fabric will keep its shape during wearing, but to maintain the original texture, the twisting process should be repeated each time the garment is laundered. After washing the garment, twist it back into a ball and machine or air dry it. Store the garment as a twisted ball, rather than hanging it on a hanger. For traveling, the twisted balls can be packed in the suitcase.

The easiest garments to sew from twisted fabric are straight-cut dresses, tunics, and T-shirts, using the entire 45" (1.15 m) width of the fabric. Instructions for sewing these simple garments are given on pages 16 and 17. Or finish the edges of a length of twisted silk with a narrow hem as on page 17, step 5, to make a scarf or belt.

How to Make Twisted Silk

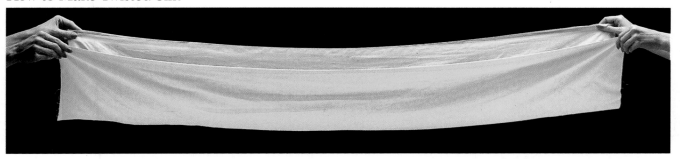

1) Cut ends of fabric on crosswise grainline. Soak fabric in lukewarm water until thoroughly wet; squeeze out excess water. Fold fabric in half lengthwise, with one person at each end of fabric; then fold in half again lengthwise.

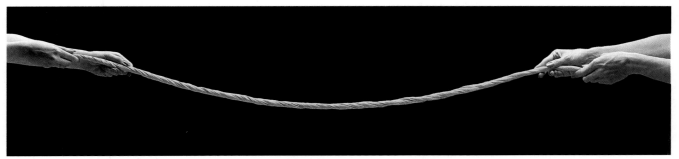

2) Gather ends of fabric in hands. Twist fabric in opposite directions, squeezing out any bubbles that form while twisting; continue until fabric is twisted as tightly as possible and begins to curl.

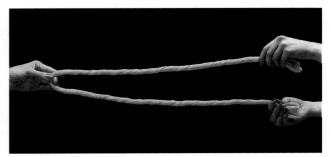

3) Fold fabric in half crosswise, with one person holding both ends and other person holding the loop.

4) Twist fabric as tightly as possible until it curls into a small, twisted ball.

5) Wrap white cotton string around ball of fabric until it is held securely and will not unwind. Take care that twisted ends of fabric are secured under string.

6) Place ball in toe of white hosiery, so ball will not unwind. Dry fabric in clothes dryer with towels; towels absorb moisture and help reduce noise. Ball of 2 to 3 yards (1.85 to 2.75 m) of fabric may take more than 3 hours to dry.

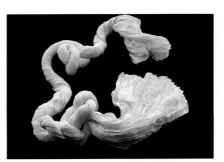

7) Insert finger into middle of ball to check for dryness. When ball is thoroughly dry, untwist fabric; if fabric is damp when untwisted, there will be unpleated areas in the finished fabric.

Sewing Garments from Twisted Silk

To sew a simple dress or blouse from twisted silk, the entire width of the 45" (1.15 m) fabric is used. You will need a length of China silk or silk broadcloth, twice the desired length of the garment plus 2" to 3" (5 to 7.5 cm) per yard (0.95 m) for shrinkage. Prepare the twisted silk fabric as on pages 14 and 15.

The neck opening of the garment can be cut to any shape. A bateau, or boat, neckline, 11" (28 cm) wide, or a round neckline, 8½" to 9½" (21.8 to 24.3 cm) wide, works well. Check to see that the neck opening is large enough for the garment to be pulled over the head easily.

How to Sew a Twisted-silk Dress or Blouse

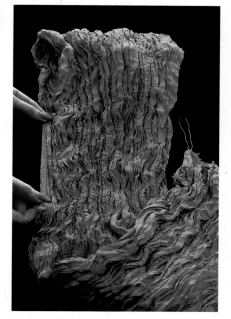

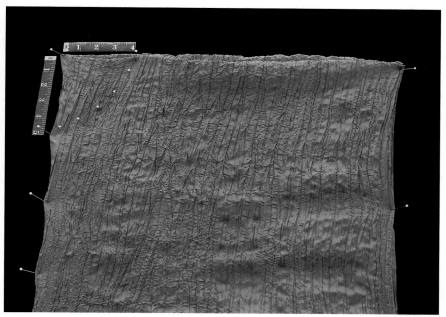

1) Fold fabric in half crosswise, right sides together, with raw edges even and selvages matching. Stitch side seams the width of selvage, stitching from raw edges to about 9" (23 cm) from foldline. Selvages remain unstitched at armholes.

2) Fold in half lengthwise on padded surface, matching side seams and crosswise folds at upper edge. Pin armholes to surface. Pull fabric to smooth out wrinkles; pin. Measure and cut neck opening. For round neckline, cut neck opening 4" (10 cm) from center fold, curving to 4" to 5" (10 to 12.5 cm) below crosswise foldline at center. For bateau neckline, cut opening 5½" (14 cm) from center fold, curving to 1½" (3.8 cm) below foldline at center.

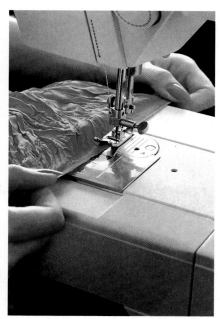

3) Baste ¼" (6 mm) from foldline at shoulders, stitching through both layers. Pull basting thread to gather shoulder seams. For a sleeveless garment, gather seams to 4½" to 5" (11.5 to 12.5 cm) length. For cap sleeves, gather seams to 7½" to 9" (19.3 to 23 cm) length.

4) Cut seam binding ¾" (2 cm) shorter than the shoulder seam; center under seamline. Stitch the shoulder seam on gathering threads, using short stitch length and catching seam binding in stitching. Tack seam allowances to one side at sleeve edge.

5) Stitch narrow hem along the neckline and hemline, using wide zigzag stitch and short stitch length, stitching off the edge of fabric slightly so edge will roll.

Acid-washed Silk

China silk, silk broadcloth, or silk charmeuse can be acid-washed, using white vinegar, to change the appearance and feel, or hand, of the fabric. The vinegar gives the fabric a sueded effect, and also helps to set the color. The silk should be soaked thoroughly in warm water before it is washed with the vinegar so the fabric will absorb the vinegar evenly, resulting in an even color throughout the acid-washed silk.

Acid-washed silk can be washed and dried by machine; little or no pressing is needed if it is removed from the dryer immediately.

Because silks may shrink 2" to 3" (5 to 7.5 cm) per yard (0.95 m), allow extra fabric when calculating yardage for your garment or project.

1) Finish raw edges of fabric. Soak fabric in warm water until thoroughly wet; squeeze out excess water.

2) Fill washing machine with hot water to a low water level. Add 2 cups (0.47 l) white vinegar; agitate a few minutes to distribute vinegar. Place fabric in machine and agitate 12 minutes; follow with the usual rinse and spin cycles.

Before and after. Before silk is acid-washed, it is shiny and smooth (top). Afterward, it has a matte or sueded appearance and a soft, suedelike hand (bottom).

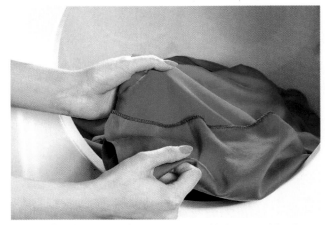

3) Dry fabric at regular setting until thoroughly dry. Repeat washing and drying once or twice, until desired effect is achieved. If pressing is required, press lightly to prevent fabric shine.

Skirt and scarf were made from unfelted fabric. The remaining fabric was felted for the jacket.

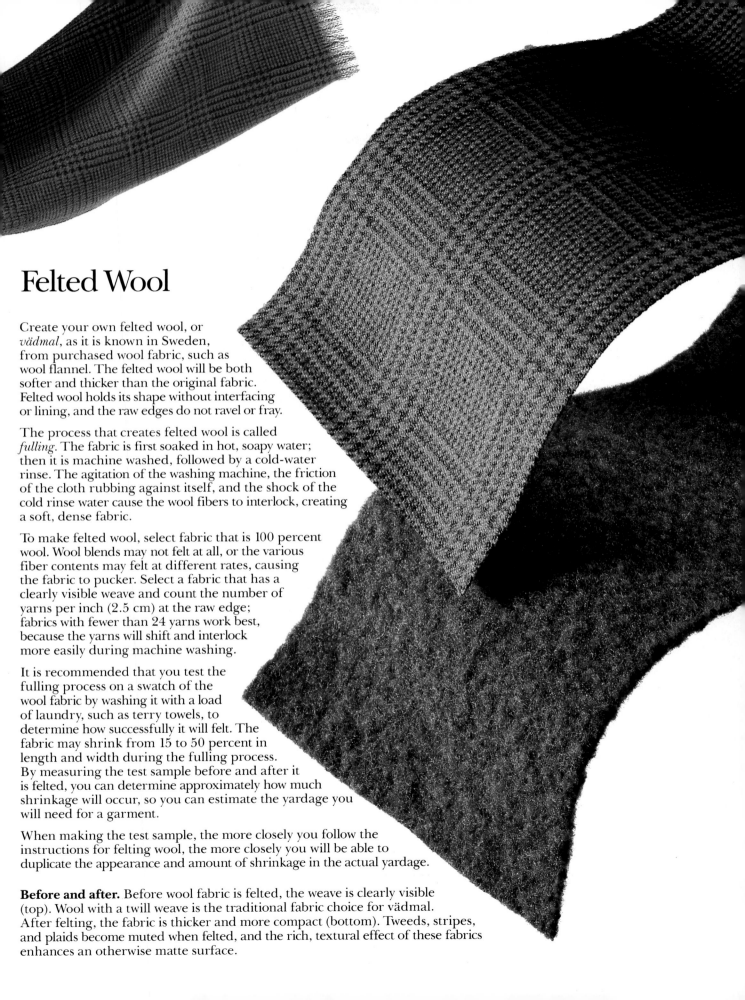

Felted Wool

Create your own felted wool, or *vädmal*, as it is known in Sweden, from purchased wool fabric, such as wool flannel. The felted wool will be both softer and thicker than the original fabric. Felted wool holds its shape without interfacing or lining, and the raw edges do not ravel or fray.

The process that creates felted wool is called *fulling*. The fabric is first soaked in hot, soapy water; then it is machine washed, followed by a cold-water rinse. The agitation of the washing machine, the friction of the cloth rubbing against itself, and the shock of the cold rinse water cause the wool fibers to interlock, creating a soft, dense fabric.

To make felted wool, select fabric that is 100 percent wool. Wool blends may not felt at all, or the various fiber contents may felt at different rates, causing the fabric to pucker. Select a fabric that has a clearly visible weave and count the number of yarns per inch (2.5 cm) at the raw edge; fabrics with fewer than 24 yarns work best, because the yarns will shift and interlock more easily during machine washing.

It is recommended that you test the fulling process on a swatch of the wool fabric by washing it with a load of laundry, such as terry towels, to determine how successfully it will felt. The fabric may shrink from 15 to 50 percent in length and width during the fulling process. By measuring the test sample before and after it is felted, you can determine approximately how much shrinkage will occur, so you can estimate the yardage you will need for a garment.

When making the test sample, the more closely you follow the instructions for felting wool, the more closely you will be able to duplicate the appearance and amount of shrinkage in the actual yardage.

Before and after. Before wool fabric is felted, the weave is clearly visible (top). Wool with a twill weave is the traditional fabric choice for vädmal. After felting, the fabric is thicker and more compact (bottom). Tweeds, stripes, and plaids become muted when felted, and the rich, textural effect of these fabrics enhances an otherwise matte surface.

How to Make a Test Sample of Felted Wool

Cut a piece of 100% wool fabric 12" (30.5 cm) long by width of fabric. Overlap and baste selvages together. Soak test sample in hot, soapy water for 30 minutes. Then wash sample with a load of laundry, such as towels, and dry it, following instructions for making felted wool as closely as possible (pages 23 to 25).

2) Measure length of felted test sample; divide by original length of sample, 12" (30.5 cm).

How to Determine Yardage of Wool Required

1) Remove basting stitches and measure width of felted test sample. Determine length required to lay out pattern on this width of fabric by referring to pattern envelope or by laying out pattern pieces on another fabric folded to this width.

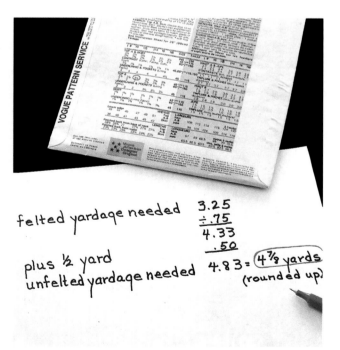

3) Divide length requirement from step 1 by result of step 2. Add ½ yard (0.50 m) to allow for possible ruffling at cut ends. This is the length of wool fabric needed for felting.

How to Make Felted Wool

1) Finish raw edges of wool, if desired. Overlap and baste selvages together to form a tube. This prevents fabric from becoming twisted around the agitator of washing machine and prevents or minimizes ruffled or uneven appearance at edges.

2) Soak fabric for 30 minutes in 100° to 120°F (42° to 49°C) hot, soapy water. This evenly wets the fabric, preventing uneven fulling, and begins to open up the wool fibers. Drain water, and remove fabric.

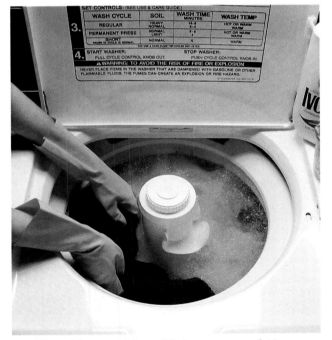

3) Fill washing machine with hot water and ½ cup (119 ml) liquid dishwashing soap. Coil wet fabric loosely around agitator. For small load, it may be necessary to add a terry towel to balance the load. Place lint filter over end of washing machine hose to collect lint.

4) Check fabric about every five minutes during wash cycle, wringing out a section to examine texture. The longer the fabric is washed, the thicker it becomes. Stop washing when desired appearance is reached. Do not felt the fabric too much; process may be repeated if more felting is desired.

(Continued on next page)

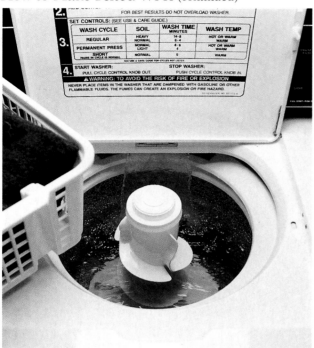

5) **Spin dry** fabric, using delicate cycle so wrinkles will not be set into fabric. Remove fabric from washing machine while cold rinse water enters machine; impact of rinse water onto fabric may cause uneven felting.

6) **Return** fabric to washing machine for cold-water rinse cycle. Spin dry, using delicate cycle for one minute or less, to remove most of the water without causing permanent wrinkles.

7) **Remove** fabric from washing machine immediately. Remove basting stitches.

8) **Shake** fabric. Remove any creases by pulling fabric sharply several times.

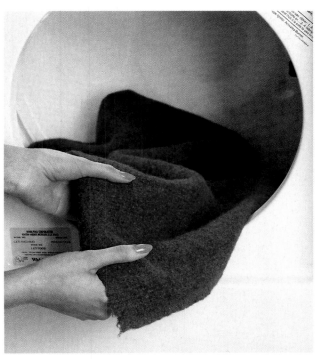

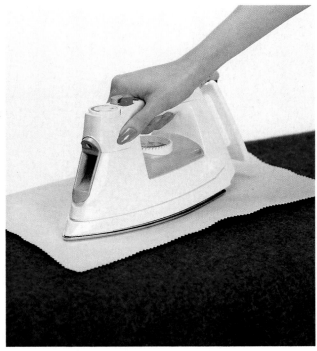

9) Machine dry fabric, using low temperature setting, if more felting is desired; check fabric frequently to prevent too much felting. Or hang fabric over heavily padded clothesline to dry.

10) Press fabric on both sides when nearly dry to the touch, using lots of steam; use press cloth or iron soleplate guard to prevent scorching or a shiny surface. Pressing helps to stabilize the fabric and smooth out the wrinkles.

11) Trim selvages from felted wool if fabric appears ruffled along selvages. If fabric is heavily felted, the selvage may not have shrunk as much as the fabric, causing ruffled appearance. Press fabric along edges after trimming selvages.

12) Hang well-pressed fabric for about 12 hours to dry completely; fabric retains a lot of moisture even after it is pressed.

Sewing Garments from Felted Wool

When sewing a garment from felted wool, select a pattern that has simple design lines. Because of the thickness of the fabric, avoid designs that have darts, pleats, or gathers. Felted wool may stretch somewhat, causing an unlined garment to conform to the contours of the body. If you want to prevent this, the felted wool garment may be lined.

For accuracy in cutting, the pattern should be laid out on a single layer of felted wool; make full-size pattern pieces, as necessary.

Use a size 90/14 or a 100/16 needle for sewing felted wools. For decorative seams and edge finishes, use topstitching thread, lightweight yarn, or other decorative thread.

Conventional seams **(a)** are sewn right sides together and pressed open. They are frequently used for a tailored appearance, although these seams may be too bulky for heavily felted wools. In conventional seams with braid trim **(b),** the seams are stitched wrong sides together, and the raw edges are covered with a trim, such as slentre braid (pages 88 and 89). Because the seams are enclosed on the inside, this method is especially suitable for unlined garments.

Lapped seams **(c)** are less bulky than conventional seams and have a sporty appearance.

Topstitched edge finishes **(d)** are usually used with lapped seams, because they are similar in appearance.

To eliminate bulk, you may want to sew single-layer collars and cuffs. The collar and cuffs may be attached to the garment using a conventional or lapped seam. The outer edges may be finished using the topstitched edge finish.

How to Sew a Conventional Seam

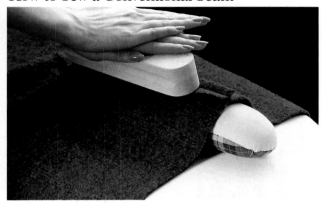

Without braid trim. Stitch seam, right sides together. Using steam, press flat; then press open over seam roll. Protect fabric with an iron soleplate guard or press cloth. Place clapper over seam; press down firmly. Hold in place until fabric is cool and dry.

With braid trim. Stitch seam, *wrong* sides together; press (left). Trim seam allowances, and cover them with braid trim. Attach braid by hand; finish ends (page 89).

How to Sew a Lapped Seam

1) Trim off seam allowance from overlapping garment section. Mark seamline on right side of underlapping garment section, using chalk or water-soluble marking pen. Apply basting tape to seam allowance.

2) Align edge of overlapping section to the marked seamline. Stitch close to the edge through all layers. Remove basting tape. Stitch again ¼" (6 mm) from first row of stitching. Trim excess seam allowance on inside of garment.

How to Sew a Topstitched Edge Finish

1) Turn under seam or hem allowance; press. Stitch a scant ⅜" (1 cm) from pressed foldline; stitch again close to edge.

2) Trim excess seam or hem allowance from wrong side of garment.

Discharge Dyeing

Discharge dyeing removes dye from fabric. This may result in a lighter shade of the original fabric color, or create an entirely different color. Designs are created on the fabric by removing the dye in certain areas and leaving the original fabric color in the remainder of the fabric. Dyes from some fabrics may not discharge well, causing little or no change in color.

One technique for discharging the dye from a fabric uses a liquid solution of one part household chlorine bleach and five parts water. The fabric is submerged in the solution until the color changes.

Another technique uses a discharge paste, made by mixing chlorine bleach and water with monagum powder, available from dye supply stores. The paste is applied to the surface of the fabric by painting it on or by screen printing.

For either technique, the bleach must be neutralized after the dye is discharged to prevent excessive damage to the fibers. Neutralize the bleach by soaking the fabric in a solution of one part white vinegar and two parts water. Then wash the fabric, using laundry detergent without bleaching agents.

Most fabrics of 100% rayon, cotton, or linen fibers work well for discharge dyeing. Do not discharge the dye from silk and wool fabrics, because they will deteriorate. Avoid using fabric blends, because it is difficult to discharge the dye from blends.

Test the discharge process on swatches of various fabrics to see which fabrics contain dyes that discharge and to see if you like the resulting color. To quickly test a fabric, apply a small amount of undiluted bleach. Within a few minutes, the color of the fabric should change. If not, apply a little more bleach; if the fabric dries before the color changes, it is not suitable.

Although bleach is a common household product, it is a toxic chemical that needs to be used with care. Use utensils and durable plastic or glass containers that are not used for food. Use bleach in a well-ventilated room, drawing the air flow away from you.

Jacket fabric has been discharge dyed using discharge paste.

Skirt fabric has been discharge dyed using liquid discharge solution.

Length of time needed to discharge the dye depends on the type of fabric and the amount of color change desired. Graduated colors can be made by varying the length of time the fabric stays in the discharge solution.

Discharge Dyeing Using a Liquid Discharge Solution

To discharge the dye from fabric, submerge it in a discharge solution of one part chlorine bleach and five parts water at room temperature. Use a sturdy plastic or glass container, large enough so the fabric can move freely when agitated. Mix a quantity of solution sufficient to cover the fabric in the container.

To make a design, the prewashed fabric can be bundled, using rubber bands, before it is submerged. You may want to experiment with different sizes of rubber bands; large, thick rubber bands create a different effect than small, thin ones. Wide latex strips, available from medical supply stores, may also be used.

Another way to make a design is with gathering threads. The fabric is gathered by pulling up rows of hand basting. The design you achieve depends on the placement of the stitches.

The length of time the fabric is left in the discharge solution affects the way the design will look. If the fabric is removed from the solution before the inside folds of the fabric become wet, there will be more color variation in the fabric. Keep in mind that the fabric will appear lighter after it is dried.

After the dye is discharged, the bleach is neutralized to prevent it from causing excessive damage to the fibers. This is done by soaking the fabric in a neutralizing solution of one part white vinegar and two parts water, then washing and rinsing it thoroughly.

How to Discharge Dye Using a Liquid Discharge Solution

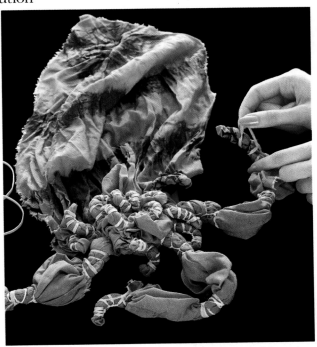

1) Prewash the fabric to remove sizing; machine dry. Bundle fabric (pages 32 and 33). Wet fabric thoroughly with clear water; gently squeeze out excess water. Mix discharge solution, opposite. Wearing rubber gloves, submerge fabric in solution, and agitate fabric gently for length of time desired, opposite.

2) Rinse the fabric thoroughly with clear, cold water, handling fabric carefully; fabric is weaker when wet. Squeeze out excess water. Remove rubber bands or gathering threads.

3) Mix neutralizing solution, opposite. Soak fabric in solution at least ½ hour, agitating it occasionally to ensure that solution penetrates all fibers. Gently squeeze out excess solution. Rinse with cold water.

4) Wash fabric thoroughly in warm water, using a mild laundry detergent without bleaching agents; rinse thoroughly. Neutralize and wash fabric again if fabric smells of bleach. If fabric smells of vinegar, wash fabric again. Line dry or machine dry fabric.

How to Bundle Fabric Using Rubber Bands or Latex Strips

Circular design. 1) Bundle fabric at center, wrapping rubber band or latex strip around fabric and twisting it on same side of bundle, as shown.

2) Continue to bundle fabric randomly, or in desired pattern. Discharge dye, using liquid discharge solution (pages 30 and 31) or discharge paste (pages 34 and 35).

Accordian-pleated design. 1) Fold dry fabric in accordian pleats. Wrap latex strips or rubber bands around pleated fabric. Discharge dye, using liquid discharge solution (pages 30 and 31) or discharge paste (pages 34 and 35).

2) Refold dry fabric in opposite direction in accordian pleats, if windowpane effect is desired. Wrap pleated fabric, as in step 1, left. Discharge dye again, using liquid discharge solution (pages 30 and 31) or discharge paste (pages 34 and 35).

How to Bundle Fabric Using Gathering Threads

Wave design. 1) Stitch planned or random wavy lines, using hand basting.

2) Pull threads to gather fabric; knot threads. Discharge dye, using liquid discharge solution (pages 30 and 31) or discharge paste (pages 34 and 35).

Diamond design. 1) Fold fabric in half lengthwise; lay flat on padded ironing surface. Fold each half evenly in accordian pleats; press folds lightly.

2) Hand-baste evenly spaced triangles at folds, through all layers, with each triangle about half the width of folded fabric; leave thread tails. Pull threads to gather fabric; wrap tails around gathers, and knot threads. Discharge dye, using liquid discharge solution (pages 30 and 31) or discharge paste (pages 34 and 35).

Discharge Dyeing Using a Discharge Paste

To discharge the dye from fabric in specific areas, use a discharge paste, made by mixing monagum powder, water, and chlorine bleach. It is easier to control the placement of discharge paste than of liquid discharge solution, allowing you to have more control over the design.

Three tablespoons (45 ml) of monagum powder are mixed with 1 cup (0.25 l) of warm water, then allowed to set for half an hour until the paste thickens and clarifies. Chlorine bleach is added to the monagum-water paste, one teaspoon at a time, until the desired strength is achieved. Check the strength of the discharge paste on a fabric swatch after each teaspoon of bleach is added, to determine how quickly the dye discharges. The less bleach is added to the paste, the gentler it will be on the fabrics.

The discharge paste may be used at room temperature. However, if the dye tends to discharge too quickly to control the color change, the paste may be chilled in the refrigerator to slow down the reaction time.

When the paste is the desired strength, check the consistency. The paste will have been thinned somewhat by adding the bleach; however, if it is still too thick, it can be thinned by adding a small amount of water.

The discharge paste can be applied to fabric that has been bundled (pages 32 and 33). Or use screen-printing techniques (pages 42 to 47) to apply the discharge paste.

The bleach is neutralized after the dye is discharged to prevent it from causing excessive damage to the fibers. This is done by soaking the fabric in a neutralizing solution of one part white vinegar and two parts water.

How to Discharge Dye Using a Discharge Paste

Bundling. 1) Mix discharge paste, opposite. Prewash fabric to remove sizing; machine dry. Bundle fabric, using rubber bands or gathering threads (pages 32 and 33). Apply discharge paste to surface of bundled areas, or to fabric between bundles.

2) Allow paste to set until desired color change occurs; keep in mind that color will be lighter after it is dried. Rinse fabric thoroughly with running water, allowing water to flush away paste; do not rub. Squeeze out excess water.

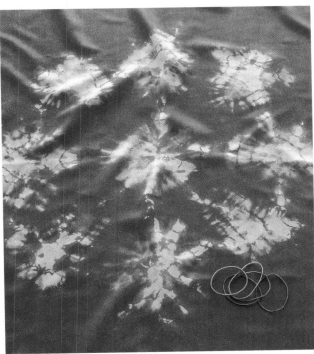

3) Remove rubber bands or gathering threads; handle fabric carefully because it is weaker when wet. Then neutralize, wash, and dry the fabric as on page 31, steps 3 and 4.

Screen printing. Mix thin discharge paste, opposite. Prewash fabric to remove sizing; machine dry. Pin onto completely dry surface. Screen print as on pages 42 to 47. Rinse as in step 2, above. Then neutralize, wash, and dry the fabric as on page 31, steps 3 and 4.

Fabric Painting

Fabrics can be painted to add an artistic touch to garments and accessories. Paints can be applied to either woven or knit fabrics. Mediumweight to heavyweight wovens are easier to paint, because they do not shift during painting. Remove any sizing from the fabric by washing it before painting. Soft leather with an unwaxed surface can also be painted. The leather may be sueded, buffed, or embossed.

Use textile paints, applying them with synthetic brushes. For a variety of interesting designs, a number of other tools, such as kitchen or sewing utensils, can be used to apply paint.

It is important to practice the painting techniques on scraps of the fabric or on paper before painting on the actual fabric. You will develop confidence as you become familiar with the materials and techniques.

Protect the work surface by covering it with a sheet of plastic. If you are painting a completed garment, such as a T-shirt, you can also place plastic between the front and back of the garment to prevent the paint from penetrating both layers.

Heat-set the paints according to the manufacturer's directions. Most heat-setting processes require a temperature of 325°F (163°C) for three minutes to remove all the moisture from the paint. Usually paint is heat-set by pressing with an iron; use a dry iron and a press cloth or brown paper when pressing leather. For items such as shoes and handbags, allow the item to air dry; then heat-set the paint with a hair dryer. After the paints have been heat-set, use the care method recommended for the fabric.

Shower curtains can be painted to complement a bathroom color scheme.

Water-repellent fabrics, such as in umbrellas, can be painted with water-based enamel; check the fabric recommendations on the label.

Accessories, such as leather handbags, can be painted to accent a special ensemble.

How to Paint Fabric in an All-over Design

1) Wet fan brush; blot excess water on a sponge or paper towel. Work bristles so fan is separated into small fingers. Dip into paint ¼" (6 mm), taking care that bristles remain separated into fingers.

2) Make several brush strokes about 1" (2.5 cm) in length on fabric, applying *light* pressure and using one color of paint. Refill brush with paint, as needed, and vary direction of brush strokes, as desired.

How to Paint Fabric in a Randomly Spaced Design

1) Wet fan brush; blot excess water on a sponge or paper towel. Coat brush with paint. Make large, curving brush strokes, 3" to 5" (7.5 to 12.5 cm) in length.

2) Wash brush; using second color of paint, make curved brush strokes, about 2" (5 cm) in length, using method in steps 1 and 2, above.

3) Wash brush. Apply a different color of paint, making fewer brush strokes than with first color.

4) Repeat step 3 for each color that is used. By layering more colors in the design, more depth is achieved.

3) Apply third color, using a medium round brush. Make small, curving brush strokes, about 1" (2.5 cm) in length; overlap some of the larger strokes.

4) Use Monoject® tool to add squiggles, as on page 40. Dip wooden end of brush in a different color of paint; add dots of paint on fabric.

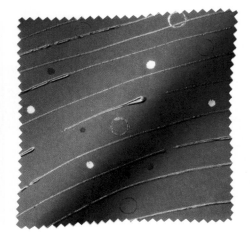

Creative Painting Techniques

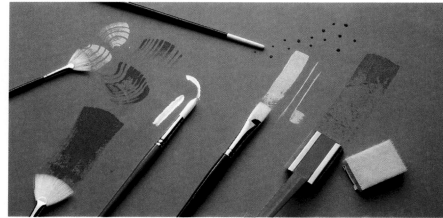

Brushes of different types and sizes are used to create different effects. Variety can also be achieved by changing the size of the brush strokes and the number of repetitions.

Sponges can print many designs. Use precut sponges, or cut shapes, using scissors or artist's knife. Dip sponge into paint. Remove excess paint, using spatula or brush.

Monoject® tool is used for swirled designs. Place tip of #412 Monoject tool into 1" (2.5 cm) of paint and pull plunger to suction paint into tube; fill one-quarter full. Wipe tip clean. Keeping tip on surface of fabric and holding tool, as shown, use *slight* pressure to eject paint. Make squiggles at beginning and end of line to control flow.

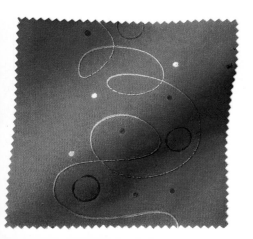

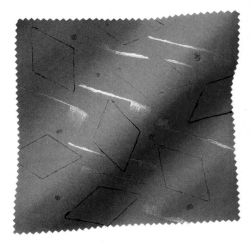

Kitchen utensils, such as wire whisk, noodle lifter, pastry edger, and cookie cutters, can be used. Bend bottom of wire whisk for a flat spiral printing surface. Do not use utensils for preparing food after using them with paint.

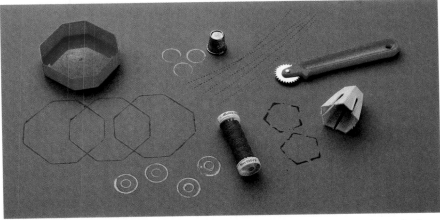

Sewing tools, including tracing wheel, thread spools, thimble, and overlock spool holders, may be used; apply paint sparingly. When using tracing wheel, coat the entire wheel with paint.

Paint pad can be used for an all-over mottled design. Apply small amount of paint to end of damp pad. Apply paint to fabric in light strokes; continue until pad is dry. Brush over strokes, using pad, to mute them; allow to dry. Repeat, using additional colors of paint, if desired, blending colors into the background for muted effect; use brighter colors first.

Screen Printing

Screen printing allows you to apply a variety of designs to fabric. In screen printing, ink is forced through a fine screen onto the fabric. The sharp, clear, screen-printed designs are quick to produce. It is important to practice screen printing on test fabric to become familiar with the technique and materials.

A special type of screen is used for screen printing. Screens are easy to construct from stretcher bars and polyester mesh. A stencil, cut from Con-Tact® self-adhesive vinyl, is then placed on the screen; when the ink is applied to the screen, it passes through the open cutouts in the stencil.

Use water-based textile inks that are transparent or opaque. The ink may be heat-set, following the manufacturer's directions, for permanent designs that will withstand laundering and dry cleaning.

YOU WILL NEED

For constructing the screen:

Four stretcher bars, at least 5" (12.5 cm) longer than design.

10 xx multifilament polyester mesh.

Masking tape; duct tape, 2" (5 cm) wide; heavy-duty stapler and ¼" (6 mm) staples.

For printing the fabric:

Con-Tact® self-adhesive vinyl, artist's knife, and cutting mat.

Water-based textile inks that are transparent or opaque, in sufficient quantity for entire project.

Fabric, prewashed, cut to desired size, and pressed.

Squeegee, ½" (1.3 cm) narrower than inside measurement of frame.

Plastic sheets large enough to protect work area, newsprint, paper towels, terry towel.

Designs can be adapted from a wallpaper border or other source to make coordinating accessories, such as the duvet cover and window shade. You can vary the scale of a design by enlarging it, using a photocopy machine. Mix larger and smaller designs to add interest to a project.

How to Construct a Screen for Screen Printing

1) Assemble frame from stretcher bars, making sure corners fit tightly and are squared. Cut mesh 1" (2.5 cm) larger than frame on all four sides. Center mesh over frame, aligning grainlines with sides of frame.

2) Apply masking tape to mesh, about ½" (1.3 cm) from outer edges of frame. Smooth tape, pressing from center of frame to ends.

3) Staple mesh to frame on one side through masking tape, working from center to ends; place the staples perpendicular to edge of frame, or at a slight diagonal.

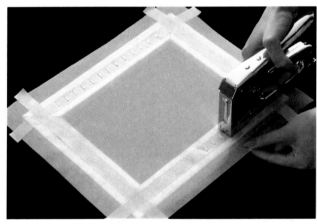

4) Staple mesh to opposite side of frame, pulling mesh tight. Repeat for other two sides. Staple corners.

5) Trim excess mesh. Apply duct tape over masking tape and staples, wrapping tape around sides of frame.

6) Apply duct tape to upper side of screen to form a border, or trough, applying about ½" (1.3 cm) of tape to mesh and remainder of tape to frame. Stencil design must fit within taped area.

How to Prepare the Design for Screen Printing

1) Draw or photocopy desired design; design may be enlarged or reduced, using photocopy machine.

2) Hold design up to light source, such as light table or window, and trace design onto paper backing of self-adhesive vinyl.

3) Cut self-adhesive vinyl on design lines, using artist's knife.

4) Remove paper backing carefully. Apply vinyl to underside of screen, overlapping duct tape border. Apply cutout details, if any.

5) Turn screen over and press down firmly on mesh; take care to secure cut edges of stencil.

How to Screen Print the Fabric

1) Place plastic sheet over work area, including table and floor. Hang a clothesline to dry prints, if desired.

2) Place terry towel on table over plastic sheet; the padded surface helps to produce a better print. Place sheet of newsprint over towel. Place fabric, right side up, over newsprint. Position screen over fabric.

3) Place 2 to 3 tablespoons (30 to 45 ml) of ink along vinyl next to design area or along border. Applying firm, even pressure, use squeegee to pull ink back and forth across screen until ink is evenly distributed. Too many repetitions cause ink to soak through fabric; too few cause design to look uneven and incomplete.

4) Lift screen slowly to a low angle, taking care that ink does not run onto fabric; carefully peel off fabric. Between prints, rest the screen so one edge is slightly elevated, and rest the squeegee on a stand or lid. Set the screen-printed fabric aside to dry, or hang on a clothesline.

How to Clean the Screen

Clogged screen. Wipe top of screen gently, using dry facial tissue, if print is uneven or incomplete.

Final cleanup. Remove stencil from screen; wash screen as soon as printing is finished, using soft cloth. Wash off stencil and affix to waxed paper for reuse, if desired.

Print is uneven or incomplete. Too much time may have been taken between prints, or ink may be too thick, causing clogged screen. Thin ink, if necessary, following manufacturer's directions. Wipe clogged screen, opposite.

Ink runs into fabric along edges of design. Ink was thinned too much, or stencil was not pressed firmly to the screen at edges of design.

Print has uneven patches of color. Ink was applied unevenly, or squeegee was not pulled across screen enough times.

Ink soaks into fabric. Too much ink was used, or the squeegee was pulled across screen too many times.

Creative Seams

Seams are a necessity in any garment, but they also provide opportunities for creativity. With unusual seaming techniques, ordinary garments become unique. These creative techniques may be used for the existing seams on a pattern or for seams you have added (page 62).

Stitch seams so the seam allowances are on the outside of the garment, then fringe or fray them for a decorative effect. Or plan the placement of the selvage along a seamline, and overlap the seam so the selvage shows. Or use a contrasting fabric as the binding for bound and lapped seams.

Frayed seams (left) are stitched wrong sides together, and the edges are then frayed by laundering, for a textured effect.

Edgestitched seams allow the inside of a reversible fabric to be seen along the seamlines for an interesting contrast. The seams are stitched wrong sides together; then the seam allowances are turned under and edgestitched.

Fringed seams offer textural interest along the seamlines. Straight-grain seams are stitched wrong sides together; then the fabric is raveled to make the fringe.

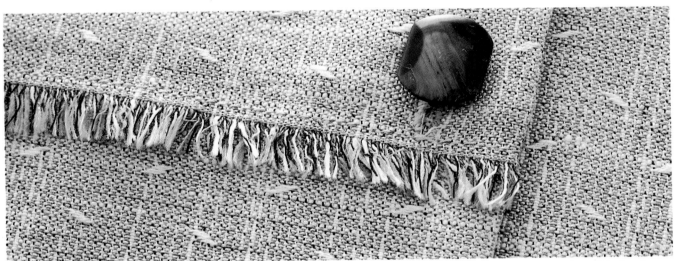

Lapped seams with exposed selvages have the look of a coordinating trim. This technique is used on fabrics that have interesting selvages.

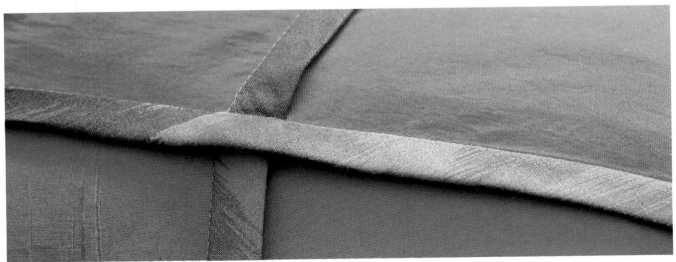

Bound and lapped seams are stitched with contrasting binding fabric for a decorative look.

Frayed Decorative Seams

To achieve the textural effect of frayed decorative seams, the garment is washed and dried several times, until the cut edges curl and fray.

Frayed seams work best on fabrics that are 100 percent cotton or silk, including cotton or silk broadcloth, cotton flannel, and denim, but other machine-washable fabrics may be used.

Before sewing the garment, you may want to make a test sample of a seam and launder the sample to see how the fabric frays.

The same basic technique may be used to make frayed trims from strips of fabric. The trims may be made from several layers of fabric for a fuller texture.

Frayed trim can be applied in rows for a sporty effect.

How to Sew a Frayed Decorative Seam

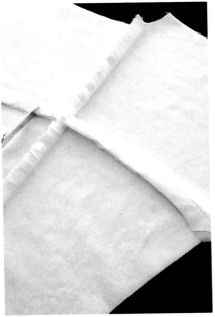

1) Cut garment sections with desired seam allowances, from ⅜" to 2" (1 to 5 cm) wide. At the end of any seam that will be intersected by another frayed seam, cut out a square the width of the seam allowance to eliminate bulk.

2) Stitch seams, with wrong sides together and raw edges even. Clip the seam allowances to within ⅛" (3 mm) of seamline; space clips ¼" to 1" (6 mm to 2.5 cm) apart.

3) Wash and dry the garment by machine until desired curling and fraying is achieved.

How to Sew Frayed Trims

1) Mark trim placement lines on garment section. Cut one to three fabric strips for each row of trim, with length of each strip equal to length of placement line, and width two times the finished width of trim.

2) Layer strips; baste lengthwise along center, through all layers. Fold strips in half lengthwise; press. Position strip on garment section, aligning fold to placement line; pin strip in place.

3) Stitch through all layers, close to fold. Remove basting. Clip all layers of trim to within ⅛" (3 mm) of stitching line; space clips ¼" to 1" (6 mm to 2.5 cm) apart. Wash and dry garment, as in step 3, above.

Edgestitched Seams

Edgestitched seams are effective on reversible fabrics, because the inside of the fabric is exposed at the seams. Used on French terry, the seams add a subtle contrast in texture; on double-faced fabrics, the second color at the seams can be even more of a contrast. Edgestitched seams are easiest to sew on straight seams, but may be used on seams with slight curves. For garments with sleeves, select a pattern that has a raglan or dropped set-in sleeve.

Casings, seam allowances, or hem allowances can be turned to the outside of the garment and edgestitched for a coordinated edge finish.

How to Sew an Edgestitched Seam

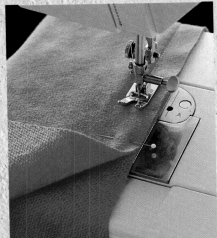

1) Cut ⅝" (1.5 cm) seams. Mark notches and construction symbols with water-soluble marking pen or chalk, instead of clipping. Stitch seams, with wrong sides together and raw edges even.

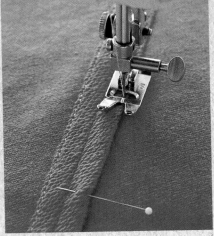

2) Press seams open. Turn seam allowances under, half the width of seam allowance. Press; pin in place. On curves, stitch ¼" (6 mm) from raw edges and clip to stitching for easier turning. Stitch close to folded edges through all layers.

How to Sew a Coordinated Edge Finish

Press casing, seam allowance, or hem allowance to right side. Turn under raw edge; press. Stitch as in step 2, left.

Fringed Seams

Fringed seams add an interesting texture at the seamlines. They can only be used for seams that are on the straight of grain, such as yokes and plackets, or at the center front or center back of a garment.

For a coordinated look on collars, faced edges, or enclosed seams, a self-fabric fringed trim can be sewn into a curved or straight seam.

Fringe a small piece of fabric as a test before making the garment, because the lengthwise and crosswise yarns in the fabric are frequently of different weights or colors, causing the fringe to look different in each direction. You may find that the varied looks of the fringe are appealing, or you may decide to fringe only those seams that run in the same direction.

Fringed trim, made from fabric strips, can be inserted in enclosed seams for a decorative effect. For a fuller effect, layer two fabric strips.

How to Sew a Fringed Seam

1) Cut out the garment, allowing ¾" (2 cm) seam allowances. Stitch seam, *wrong* sides together and raw edges even. Press seam flat.

2) Trim the seam allowance that will not be fringed, to ⅛" (3 mm).

3) Press ¾" (2 cm) seam allowance over trimmed seam allowance. Topstitch ¼" (6 mm) from seamline, using short stitch length.

4) Ravel threads from raw edge to topstitching; clip seam allowance to stitching about every 6" (15 cm), to make fringing easier.

How to Sew a Fringed Trim in an Enclosed Seam

1) Cut a fabric strip on straight of grain, with length of strip equal to length of seamline, and width equal to finished width of fringe plus ⅝" (1.5 cm) seam allowance.

2) Insert strip between garment section and facing, aligning raw edges. Stitch seam, using short stitch length; grade and clip the seam allowances.

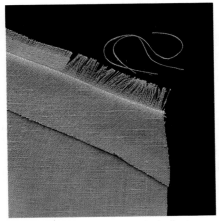

3) Press seam. Understitch facing seam, taking care not to catch strip in stitching. Clip seam allowance to stitching about every 6" (15 cm). Ravel threads to seamline.

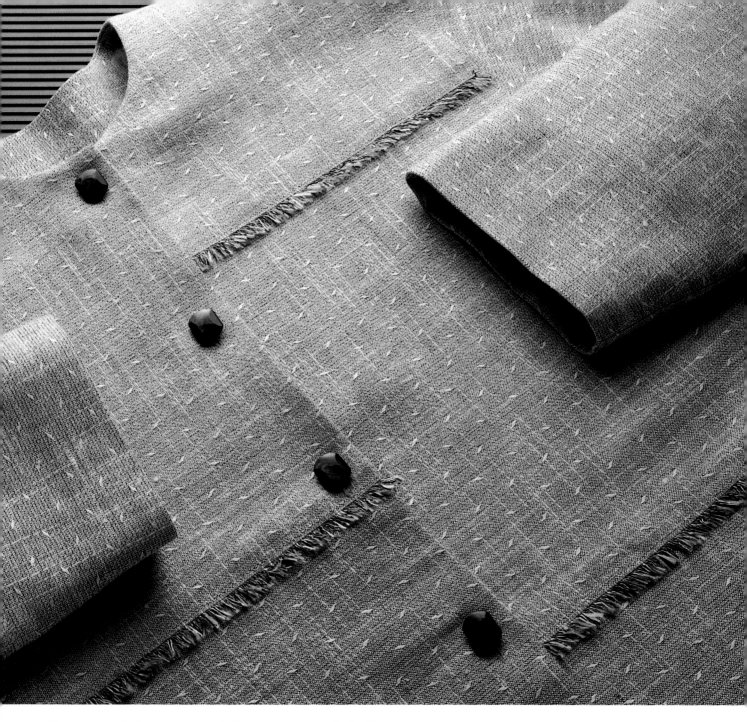

Lapped Seams with Exposed Selvages

Some fabrics have attractive selvages that you may want to feature as a trim. The exposed selvages can be used to accent existing seamlines or seamlines you have added to the pattern (page 62).

This method is limited to straight seams or edges that are cut on the lengthwise grain. Changing the grainline allows this technique to be used for vertical, horizontal, or diagonal seams.

For a selvage finish at a straight hemline, center front opening, or pocket edge, eliminate the seam or hem allowance, and place the seamline or hemline on the selvage when cutting out the pattern.

Before using this method, preshrink the fabric to see whether the selvage shrinks more than the fabric, causing it to draw up and pucker. Preshrink washable fabric as recommended in the fabric care instructions; preshrink fabric that requires dry cleaning by steaming it evenly with a steam iron and allowing it to dry thoroughly on a flat surface.

How to Sew a Seam with an Exposed Selvage

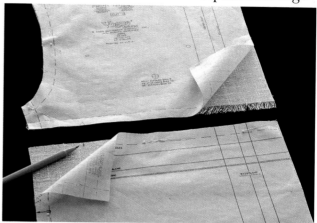

1) Cut one garment section on the selvage, eliminating seam allowance; for fringed selvages, fringe may extend beyond seamline. Cut other garment section with ⅝" (1.5 cm) seam allowance; this seam allowance will underlap the selvage. Mark notches, using water-soluble marking pen or chalk.

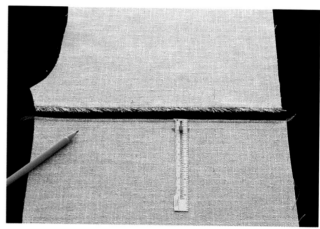

2) Mark seamline of underlap section ⅝" (1.5 cm) from raw edge. Finish seam allowance of underlap.

3) Align selvage with marked seamline; pin in place. Topstitch through selvage and underlap.

Selvages may have a decorative fringed appearance and matching or contrasting tightly woven yarns.

width six times finished width plus ¼" (6 mm). Press binding in half lengthwise; place on the right side of garment, raw edges even. Stitch seam, with seam allowance the finished width of binding.

Adding Seams for Interest

A basic garment design can become more interesting with the addition of one or more seams. When several seams are added, the new garment sections that are created can be cut from several different fabrics. A patchwork effect can be achieved with a variety of fabrics in different prints or textures. Or try color blocking by using a different color of fabric for each garment section.

Make a copy of the pattern that you can mark and cut apart when adding the new seams. Draw the seamlines on the new pattern, and check the seam placement by pin-fitting the pattern. Then cut the pattern apart and add seam allowances.

How to Add Seams to a Pattern

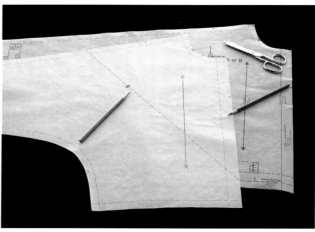

1) Trace pattern piece onto tissue paper. Draw desired new seamlines on new pattern. Mark notches to indicate where garment sections are to be matched during stitching.

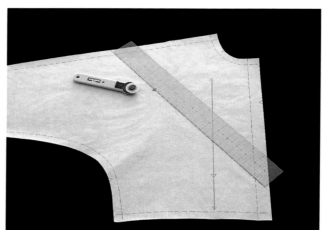

2) Extend the grainline on each new pattern section, or mark a new grainline parallel to the original. Cut pattern apart on the new seamlines.

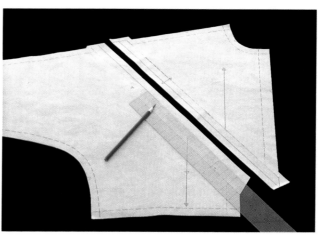

3) Add tissue paper at new seamlines; mark width of desired seam allowances. Extend notches to cutting lines of pattern.

Double & Triple Piping

Double and triple piping can be an effective way to enhance a simple garment, by accenting the design lines. The piping can be used as an edge finish or sewn into a seamline.

Bias fabric strips, cut 1½" (3.8 cm) wide, are used to cover the cording. The length of each strip should equal the combined lengths of the seams or edges to be piped plus extra for seam allowances; piece strips together, as necessary.

Rattail cord is recommended for the cording, because it provides a firm edge and is less likely to be caught by the zipper foot when the piping is stitched.

For best results, use an adjustable zipper foot so you can control how close you stitch to the piping. Tighten the fixing screw of the zipper foot firmly so the foot does not shift and break a needle. Or, if your machine has an adjustable needle position, align the needle with the zipper foot.

To make the piping, thread the machine with thread to match the color of the piping that will be on the outer edge; use this color for stitching all rows of piping.

How to Make Double and Triple Piping

1) Cut bias fabric strips, opposite; piece the strips together, as necessary. Press seams open.

2) Position zipper foot on right side of needle; adjust foot or needle position so needle is close to inside curve of opening on foot. Tighten fixing screw firmly.

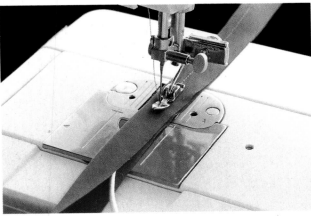

3) Fold strip that will be on outer edge around cording, with wrong sides together and raw edges even. Secure cording to end of strip, using a pin. Stitch, guiding cording along edge of foot.

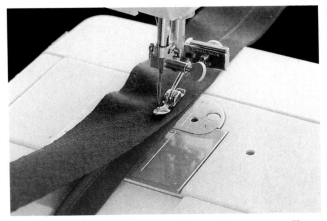

4) Adjust zipper foot or needle position so needle is aligned to *edge* of foot; tighten fixing screw firmly. Place second strip over piping, right sides together, aligning raw edges. Stitch as close as possible to cording.

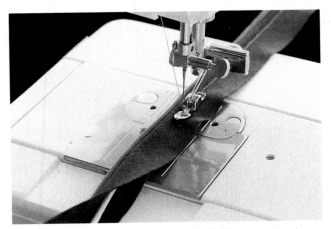

5) Adjust zipper foot as in step 2. Fold second strip around cording, and secure end with a pin; raw edges will not match. Stitch, guiding cording along edge of zipper foot.

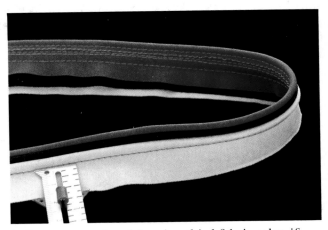

6) Repeat steps 4 and 5, using third fabric color, if triple piping is desired. Trim seam allowances of piping, if necessary, to match those of garment.

Applying Double & Triple Piping

Double and triple piping can be used at seamlines or garment edges. They should not be used around sharp corners, but may be used for rounded corners.

When used at a seamline, the piping is applied to one garment section; then the seam is stitched, and the piping laps over the other section. Determine the direction in which you want the piping to lap, so it is applied to the correct garment section. As a general rule, princess or side front seams are lapped toward the sides of a garment, side seams are lapped toward the garment back, and horizontal seams are lapped downward.

If the piping is being used at garment edges, collars, and cuffs, the facing or lining is attached by hand, concealing the rows of stitching on the underside of the piping for a neater edge finish.

How to Insert Double or Triple Piping into a Seam

1) Pin piping to garment, with right sides together and raw edges even. Adjust zipper foot as on page 65, step 2. Stitch, guiding cording along edge of foot.

2) Adjust zipper foot as on page 65, step 4. Place garment sections right sides together, with raw edges even. Stitch seam as close as possible to cording. (Presser foot has been raised to show detail.)

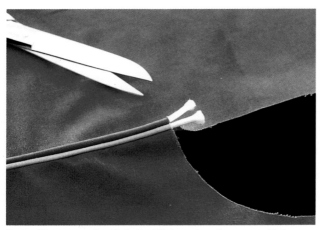

3) Pull out cords slightly, if the piped seam will be intersected by another seam or turned back at a hemline; clip ends the width of seam allowance.

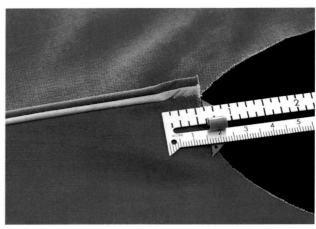

4) Pull seam to return cords to original position. Stitch intersecting seam, using zipper foot.

How to Apply Double or Triple Piping at an Edge

1) Cut facings and lining pieces, following pattern. Decrease size of pattern for garment section at seamline by width of piping; add seam allowance. Cut the garment section from adjusted pattern.

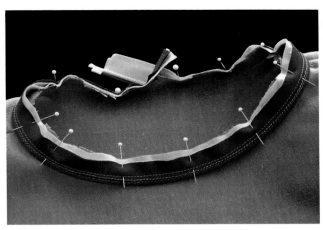

2) Pin piping to garment, with right sides together and raw edges even.

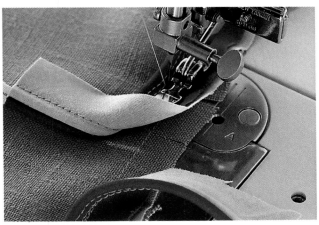

3) Adjust zipper foot as on page 65, step 4. Stitch seam, stitching as close as possible to cording; on circular edge, leave 1" (2.5 cm) unstitched at each end. Grade seam allowances and clip curves.

4) Pull up cords slightly, if necessary, for smooth inside curve. For circular edge, overlap piping and curve ends into seam allowance, so ends taper to raw edge; stitch.

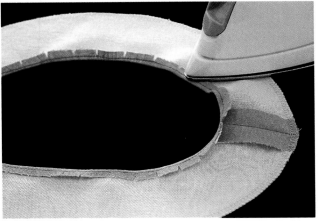

5) Stitch facing or lining piece on seamline. Trim seam allowance and clip curves. Press under facing or lining ⅛" (3 mm) beyond stitching.

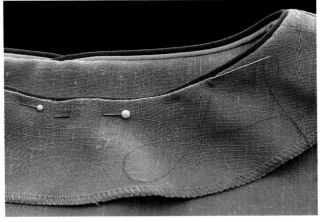

6) Pin facing to garment section so folded edge is aligned to stitching line at outer row of piping; slipstitch along folded edge.

Pockets

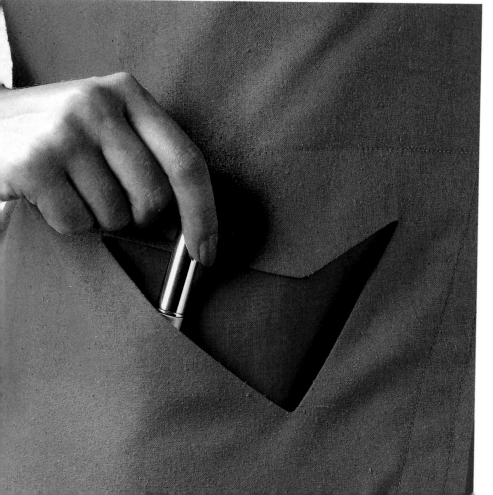

Design your own creative pockets to enhance the style of a garment, making the pockets any shape or size desired. To add even more interest, sew the pockets from contrasting fabric.

Window Pockets

Window pockets (above and left) are inventive and easy to sew, and can be used for either lined or unlined garments. The pockets can be varied by changing the size or shape. Contrasting fabric may be used for the pocket piece, to emphasize the pocket opening.

Foldover Pockets

On lined foldover pockets, the top of the pocket folds back to make a contrasting flap. Plan the shape of the pocket to complement the fabric or garment design. The pocket shapes on the garments above mimic the designs in the print fabric and the shape of the neckline. Or the pocket can repeat the shape of other garment details; for example, the notched pocket at right may be used for a garment with notched lapels.

How to Sew a Window Pocket

1) Draw desired size and shape of pocket on paper, drawing pocket opening and placement lines for topstitching.

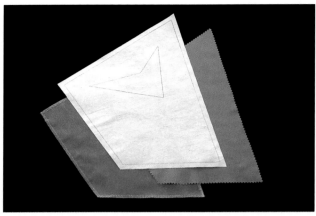

2) Make a tissue pattern, drawing cutting lines ⅜" (1 cm) outside topstitching lines. Cut one piece from lining, wrong side up. Cut another piece from matching or contrasting fabric, right side up; this piece will show at pocket opening. Finish edges.

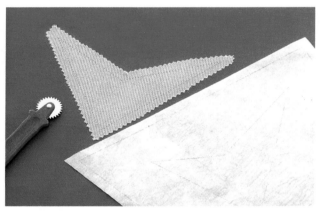

3) Mark mirror image of pocket opening on right side of fusible interfacing. Cut fusible interfacing ½" (1.3 cm) larger than pocket opening, using pinking shears. Fuse interfacing to wrong side of garment section at desired position.

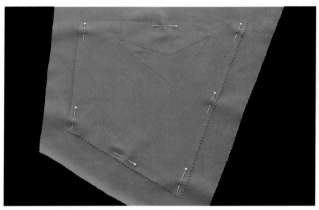

4) Position pocket lining on garment, right sides together; pin in place. Stitch through all layers, from wrong side, following marked lines for pocket opening.

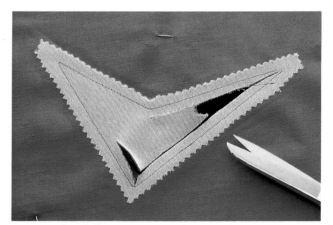

5) Trim fabric layers ¼" (6 mm) inside stitching lines; clip as necessary.

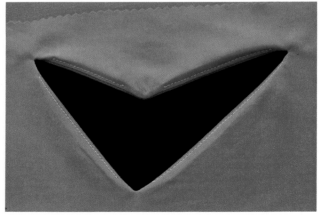

6) Turn pocket lining to wrong side of garment; press. Understitch edge of opening to prevent lining from showing on right side.

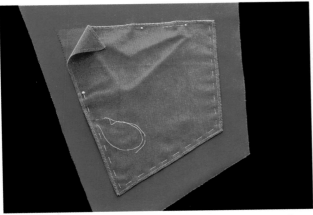

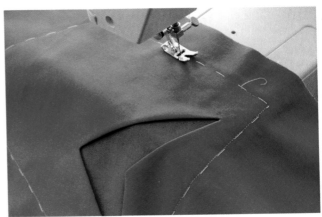

7) Position pocket piece, right side down, over pocket lining; baste from wrong side ⅜" (1 cm) from edges of pocket piece.

8) Topstitch around pocket from right side, along basting stitches. Remove basting.

How to Sew a Foldover Pocket

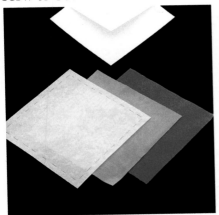

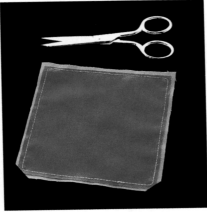

1) Design pocket, and cut the shape from paper in actual size; fold flap to check design. Make pattern from tissue, adding seam allowances. Cut one piece from each of two fabrics.

2) Place pieces right sides together, and pin. Stitch around edges; do not leave an opening. Trim corners and seam allowances; clip curves.

3) Cut small slash in lining close to lower edge. Turn pocket right side out, through slash.

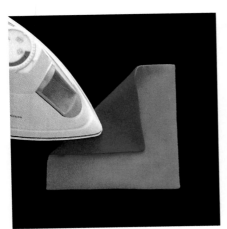

4) Press seam so lining does not show on lower pocket and outer fabric does not show on flap. Press flap.

5) Fuse slashed opening closed, using piece of fusible interfacing.

6) Pin pocket to garment; topstitch in place, backstitching at each end of pocket opening.

71

Triangular Pockets & Buttonholes

Triangular buttonholes are a variation of the couture bound buttonhole. These novelty buttonholes can be the main focal point of a garment when sewn in contrasting fabric, or can add a subtle finishing touch when sewn in matching fabric. The fabric piece for the buttonhole is cut on the straight of grain, resulting in chevroned stripes when a striped fabric is used, as shown on page 111.

To determine the length of the buttonhole opening, add the diameter of the button plus the thickness and an extra ⅛" to ¼" (3 to 6 mm) for ease. Make test samples of the buttonhole to check the fit of the button and to master the technique before sewing buttonholes on the actual garment.

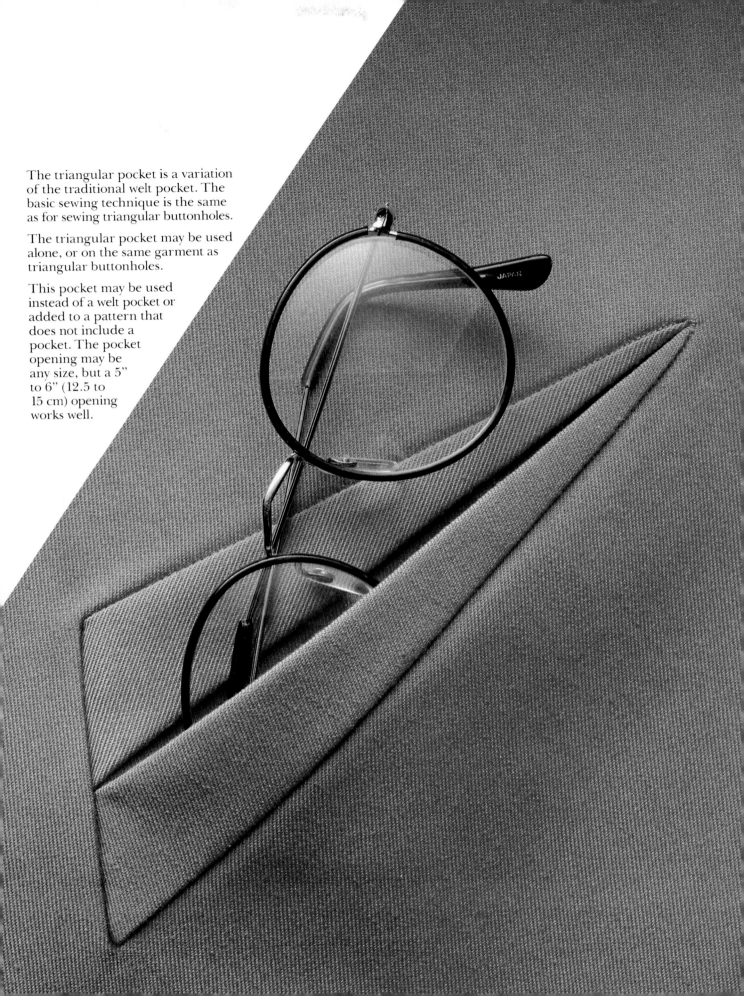

The triangular pocket is a variation of the traditional welt pocket. The basic sewing technique is the same as for sewing triangular buttonholes.

The triangular pocket may be used alone, or on the same garment as triangular buttonholes.

This pocket may be used instead of a welt pocket or added to a pattern that does not include a pocket. The pocket opening may be any size, but a 5" to 6" (12.5 to 15 cm) opening works well.

How to Sew a Triangular Bound Buttonhole

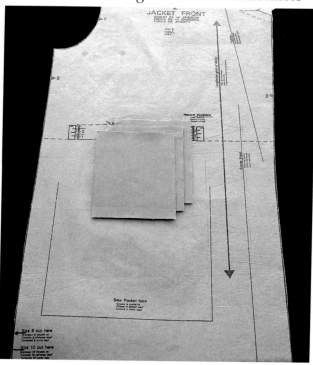

1) Plan shape and size of buttonholes. Cut a straight-grain fabric patch for each buttonhole, with length 2" (5 cm) longer than buttonhole opening and width four times finished width of buttonhole at wide end.

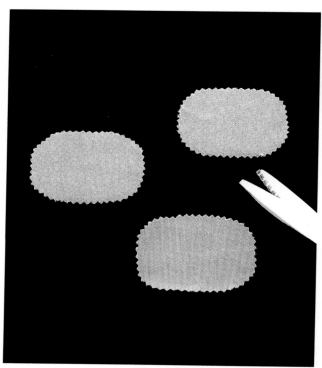

2) Cut a piece of fusible interfacing for each buttonhole, 1" (2.5 cm) longer and wider than finished triangle, using pinking shears.

3) Mark points of triangular buttonhole on garment, using tailor's tacks. Remove all but one strand of each tailor's tack. On wrong side of garment section, center interfacing over buttonhole; fuse interfacing in place.

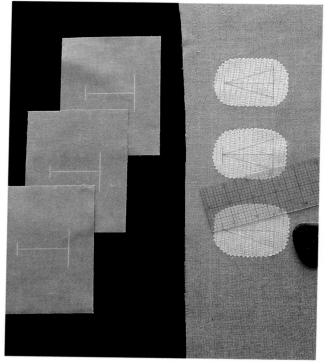

4) Mark center and ends of each buttonhole on the interfacing and wrong side of patch, using chalk. Mark lines of triangles on interfacing.

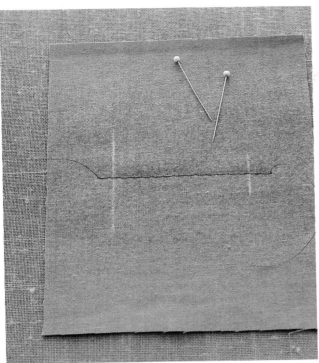

5) Place patch on garment section, right sides together, using pins to align markings. Machine-baste through center marking.

6) Stitch around marked triangle, using 20 stitches per inch (2.5 cm); begin on one side of triangle, and take one or two stitches across each point. Remove basting.

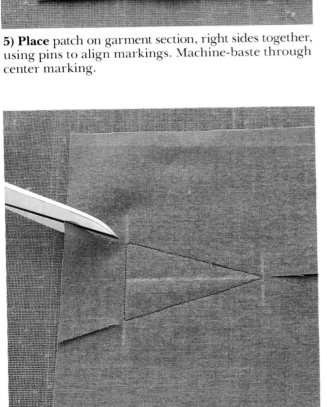

7) Cut three slashes through patch only, cutting from outer edge of patch to within ⅛" (3 mm) of corners of triangle, as shown.

8) Cut patch and garment section through center of buttonhole, stopping ¼" (6 mm) from widest end. Clip to, but not through, corners.

(Continued on next page)

9) Turn patch at wide end of buttonhole to wrong side; press seam at wide end.

10) Press patch toward buttonhole opening on two remaining seamlines.

11) Turn sides of patch to wrong side; wrap around center opening to form lips of buttonhole. Press from right side, taking care that lips are even.

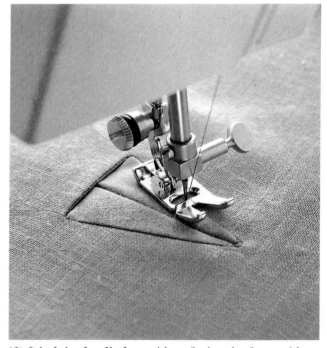

12) Stitch in the ditch on sides of triangle, from wide end to point, using matching thread and short stitch length; stitch in place at ends to secure stitches.

13) Turn garment back on itself; stitch across wide end of buttonhole over previous stitching, through all thicknesses. Trim excess fabric.

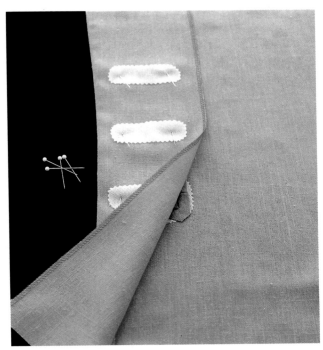

14) Attach the garment facing; press. Mark ends of buttonhole openings on facing, using pins. Cut a piece of fusible interfacing for each buttonhole, 1" (2.5 cm) longer than opening and 1" (2.5 cm) wide. Center interfacing, fusible side up, over pin-marked openings on right side of facing.

15) Mark opening on interfacing, using pencil. Mark oval shape, tapering from ends of buttonhole to ⅛" (3 mm) from marked line at center of buttonhole. Stitch around oval through interfacing and facing, taking two stitches across each end.

16) Slash on center line. Turn interfacing to wrong side of facing. Press seamlines with tip of iron; fuse interfacing in place. Slipstitch facing to garment section around oval opening.

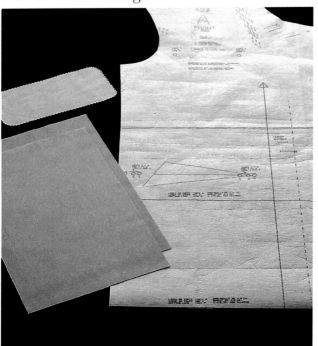

1) Cut two pieces of straight-grain fabric for pocket, with width of piece 2" (5 cm) longer than pocket opening, and length four times finished width of triangle at wide end plus 3" (7.5 cm). Cut a piece of fusible interfacing 1" (2.5 cm) longer and wider than finished triangle, using pinking shears.

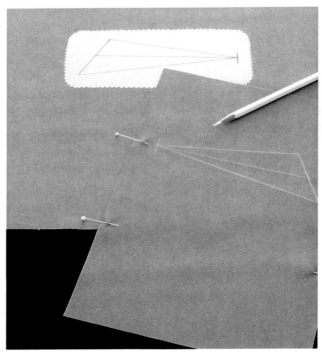

2) Mark points of triangle on garment and apply interfacing as in step 3, page 74. Mark pocket opening on interfacing; mark lines of triangle. Divide the length of one pocket piece into thirds, and pin-mark. Mark pocket opening on wrong side of pocket piece, one-third down from top; mark lines of triangle.

3) Follow steps 5 to 11, pages 75 and 76. Stitch in the ditch on lower side of triangle, from wide end to point, using matching thread and short stitch length; stitch in place at ends to secure stitches.

4) Center second pocket piece over first piece, on wrong side. Pin pocket pieces together.

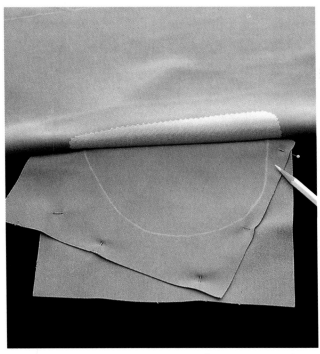

5) Place garment right side up. Lift garment section to expose lower ends of pocket pieces. Mark curved stitching line for pocket bag, starting and ending at ends of pocket opening.

6) Stitch across pointed end of triangle to reinforce point. Continue stitching on marked line around pocket bag.

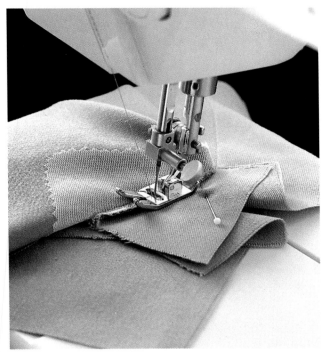

7) Continue stitching across wide end of pocket opening over previous stitching, through all thicknesses.

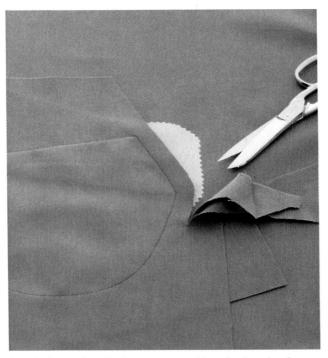

8) Stitch in the ditch on upper side of triangle, from wide end to point, using matching thread and short stitch length; stitch in place at ends to secure stitches. Trim excess fabric around pocket bag; finish edge.

Buttons in a variety of sizes, shapes, or colors can be used as a decorative detail.

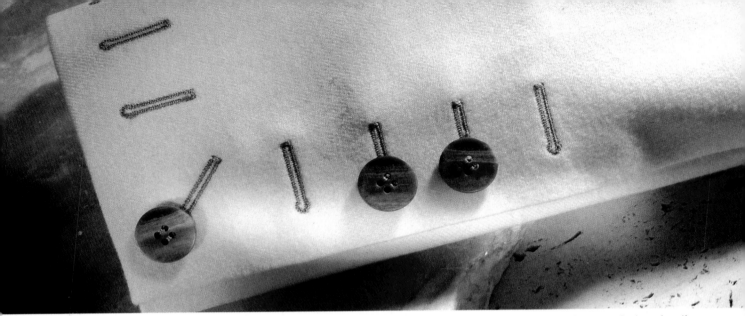

Buttonholes do not have to be functional. They can be stitched along a placket or any garment edge as a design detail.

Unexpected Creative Details

Doing the unexpected can offer many possibilities for creativity. Although most notions have been invented to serve a specific purpose, they can also be used in unconventional ways. For example, tassle fringe or gimp cord, designed as home decorating trims, can be used to accent the design details of a garment. Zipper tapes can be inserted into seams so the zipper teeth create an interesting piping, or the zipper tapes can be topstitched to a garment as a decorative, colorful trim. Buttons and buttonholes can be purely decorative rather than being used as closures.

Tassle fringe can be used to accent the lapel or neckline of a garment.

Zipper teeth can become a decorative piping to accent the edges or details of a garment; insert the zipper tape into the seam as for beaded piping (page 93).

Ribbonwork

Diagonal ribbonwork can be used to accent a jacket lapel.

Ribbonwork, an heirloom technique, can be used creatively on today's sewing projects. Many different effects can be achieved, depending on the type of ribbon used, its width, and placement.

Grosgrain, double-faced satin, and other reversible ribbons can be used for ribbonwork. Ribbons found at estate sales or in old sewing baskets can add a special heirloom effect. If you plan to wash the project, use ribbons that are washable. Check ribbons for colorfastness and shrinkage, especially old ribbons or those of unknown fiber content. The width of the ribbon may vary, depending on the effect you want.

Ribbons ⅜" or ½" (1 or 1.3 cm) wide work well, but narrower or wider ribbons can also create interesting designs. Plan the design, keeping in mind where the ribbon will start and end. The ends of the ribbon can be turned under and stitched, covered by another piece of ribbon, or stitched into a seam.

For the diagonal design, the length of ribbon required depends on the width of the ribbon and how closely spaced the diagonal lines are, but usually you will need a length of ribbon about twice the depth of the design times the number of "V's" in the design. Double this amount of ribbon for the diamond design.

Diamond ribbonwork can be used to decorate a hidden placket on a blouse.

How to Sew a Diagonal Ribbonwork Design

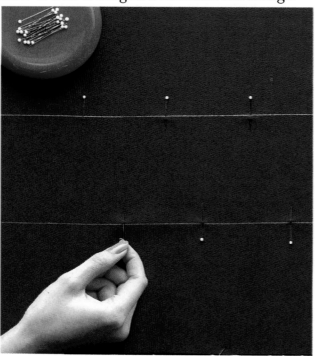

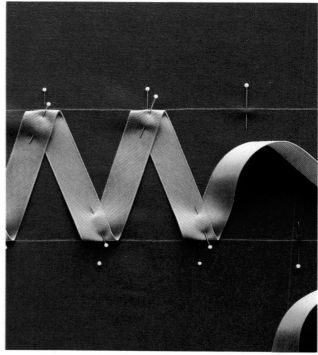

1) Mark lines for outer edges of design on fabric, using chalk or water-soluble marking pen. Plan placement of diagonal lines; mark points of diagonal lines an equal distance apart, using pins.

2) Attach reversible ribbon to fabric, using pins, folding ribbon *under* at each pin mark; align folds to outer edges, with centers of folds at pin marks. Glue-baste ribbon, if desired, to prevent shifting.

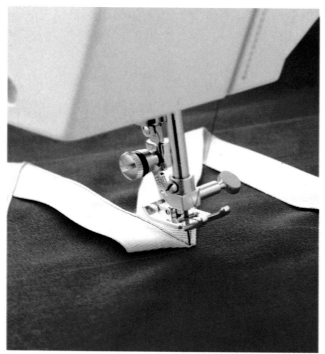

3) Stitch along overlapping edge of ribbon to fold, as shown, using matching thread or fine monofilament nylon thread. Pivot at fold, and stitch to opposite fold. Continue stitching in this manner to end of ribbon. (Contrasting thread was used to show detail.)

4) Stitch along other edge of ribbon to fold; stitch in place a few times to secure stitches. Raise presser foot and needle; pull thread past overlapping ribbon, as shown. Secure stitches, and stitch to opposite fold.

5) Continue stitching in this manner to end of ribbon.

6) Clip threads on right side of fabric; clip threads on wrong side, if desired.

How to Sew a Diamond Ribbonwork Design

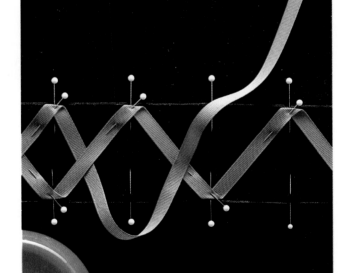

1) Mark lines and placement points, as in step 1, opposite. Pin first ribbon in place, as in step 2, opposite. Weave second ribbon alternately over and under first ribbon; pin.

2) Stitch as in steps 3 and 4, opposite, except stop stitching at intersecting ribbon; raise presser foot and needle, pull threads past intersecting ribbon, and continue stitching. Clip threads.

Slentre Braid

Slentre braid is fast and easy to make. This flexible braid has a distinctive appearance, with a half-round shape on one side and a flat, plaited look on the other. It can be made from one or several types of cord, ribbon, yarn, or narrow trim. A multicolored trim can be customized to coordinate with a specific fabric.

You may want to make a short length of slentre braid as a test sample, using one-yard (0.95 m) lengths of each of the cords or trims you are planning to use in the final project. This helps you to become familiar with the braiding technique and to check how the braid looks, before making a long piece.

To make a long, continuous braid, have an assistant help shape the braid as you interlace it.

Slentre braid may be used at seamlines or as an edge finish. When it is used at seamlines, the seams may be stitched as shown on pages 26 and 27.

How to Make Slentre Braid

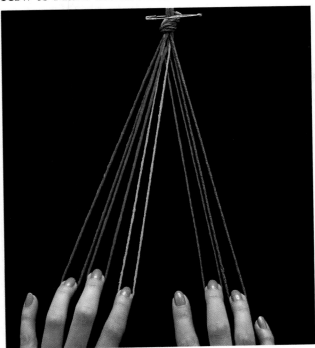

1) Cut five strands of cord; fold each in half. Tie all cut ends together; pin to padded, stationary surface, using safety pin. Hold three loops on fingers of left hand and two loops on fingers of right hand.

2) Insert index finger of right hand through middle loop on left hand, then into ring-finger loop.

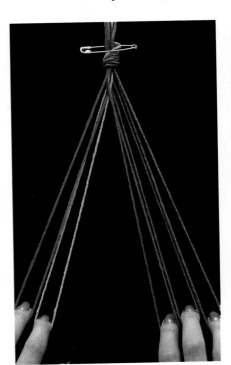

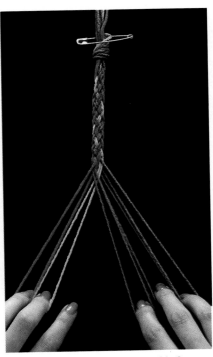

3) Draw ring-finger loop through middle loop, dropping ring-finger loop from left hand; there are now three loops on right hand and two loops on left. Pull hands apart to snug the braid in place at tied ends.

4) Shift loops on fingers of left hand by walking loops over so index finger is free. Repeat process, alternating hands until length of cord is braided.

5) Secure braid at ends by stitching across braid. Attach braid to garment by hand. To finish ends, enclose end in a seam **(a)** or fold end under just beyond stitches **(b);** stitch.

Beadwork

Glamorous beaded garments and accessories can be created, using machine sewing or handstitching techniques. Machine sewing is used to apply beading-by-the-yard, and handstitching is used to apply individual beads. A few well-placed beads can add an exquisite look to an otherwise basic item. You may want to sew a more elaborate beaded design, or make a beaded appliqué that can be attached to a garment.

Beading by Machine

Beading-by-the-yard may be applied by machine by couching over the beads with a zigzag stitch. Various types, sizes, and colors of beading-by-the-yard are available, including a few types of beaded piping.

One of the most common types of beading-by-the-yard is molded plastic pearl beading. Pearl beading should not be confused with strung pearls, which are sold on a string and applied individually by hand.

Cross-Locked™ glass beads are braided onto cotton thread; the threads form a cross on the back of each bead, resulting in evenly spaced beads. Cross-Locked glass beads are flexible, strong, and easy to handle.

Large beads are more difficult to work with, because they are less flexible. Therefore you may want to avoid using them when sewing curved designs or when attaching beads to edges.

It is recommended that you use a specialty presser foot, such as a beading or piping foot, if one is available for your sewing machine. The groove in the bottom of the presser foot must be large enough to allow the beads to ride in the groove as you sew.

An adjustable zipper foot, or any zipper foot that can be used with the zigzag stitch, can also be used for applying beading-by-the-yard. The beads are then guided along the edge of the foot. Be careful not to hit them with the needle; this can break the needle and the beads.

Fine monofilament nylon thread is excellent for applying beads by machine. It blends in with the color of the beads and fabric so it is virtually invisible. Fine machine embroidery thread may also be used.

Adjust the zigzag stitch length so a complete zigzag is equal to the distance between the beads. Adjust the stitch width so the needle will stitch over the beads without hitting them. Always test-sew, stitching slowly and turning the flywheel by hand, to be sure the needle clears the beads. You may want to practice sewing with the zigzag stitch set to the widest stitch width until you feel confident stitching over the beads; then narrow the stitch width so it is closer to the beads.

Leave a tail of beading at the beginning of the stitching line, and hold the beading and thread tails when you start to sew. To prevent puckering, hold both the fabric and the beading taut as you stitch, and loosen the needle thread tension, if necessary.

When beading is applied to smaller areas, the fabric can be held taut in an embroidery hoop. This is especially helpful when you are sewing curves.

Types of beads available by the yard include nailheads **(a)**, rhinestones **(b)**, molded plastic pearls **(c)**, and Cross-Locked glass beads **(d)**.

How to Sew Beading by Machine

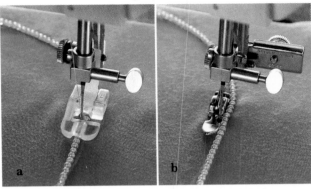

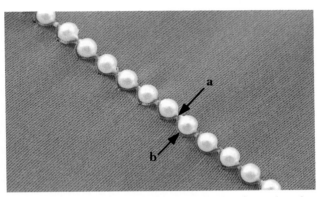

Beaded designs. 1) Mark design line on fabric to use as guide for stitching. Position beading in the groove under beading foot **(a)** or to the right of adjustable zipper foot **(b)**. Adjust zigzag stitch length and stitch width, opposite. Stitch over beads, holding fabric and beading taut as you sew.

2) Prevent puckered fabric when sewing large beads by stitching so the right swing of needle is between the beads **(a)** and the left swing of needle is next to the center of each bead **(b)**.

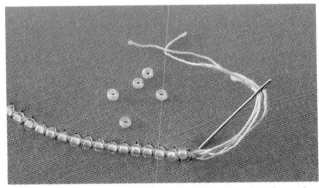

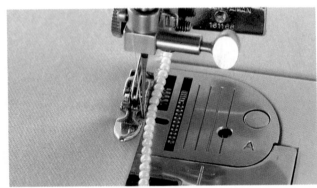

3) Secure Cross-Locked glass beads at ends of row by removing several beads and knotting the threads close to last remaining bead; thread the tails through a needle and pull to wrong side. Most other types of beading may be cut at ends without raveling.

Beaded edges. Place beading next to fabric edge. Use zipper or beading foot, and adjust stitches, opposite. Stitch over beads, so right swing of needle extends over edge of fabric between beads; left swing of needle catches fabric edge next to center of each bead. Secure ends as in step 3.

How to Insert Beaded Piping

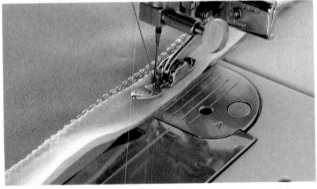

1) Place beaded piping on garment section, right sides together and raw edges even. Using zipper foot, straight-stitch close to beads. If seam allowances of garment and piping are not the same width, trim the wider seam allowance.

2) Pin facing and garment section, right sides together, with beaded piping between layers. Straight-stitch over previous stitching, using zipper foot. Trim and clip seam allowances; press.

Beading by Hand

Hand beadwork is used to apply individual beads to a garment or project. Several types of beads are available for beading by hand. A wide variety of effects can be achieved, depending on the beads that are used and how they are combined.

All beads shown here are actual size.

Pearl beads are available in many shapes and sizes.

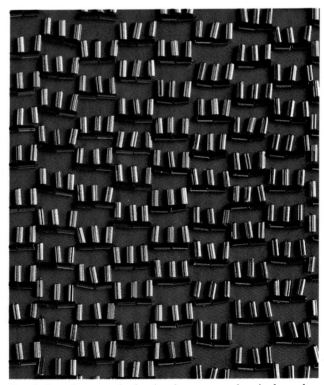

Bugle beads are tubular in shape, ranging in length from 2 to 40 mm. They may be smooth or six-sided.

Seed beads are small and round, with a center hole.

Faceted beads have flat surfaces that are cut or molded.

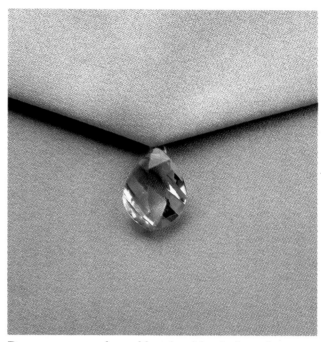

Drops are pear-shaped beads with a hole at the narrow end or lengthwise through the bead.

Fancy beads include any beads that do not fit into a specific category.

Roundels are doughnut-shaped beads, smooth or faceted. They are often used with seed beads.

Hand Beadwork

Hand beadwork is done using a beading needle, a long, fine needle with a small, round eye. The needles are available in sizes ranging from 10 to 14; the larger the number, the smaller the needle. Needles in sizes 12 and 13 are fine enough to fit through most beads, yet the eyes are large enough to be relatively easy to thread. Several beads can be threaded on a beading needle at one time. Because a beading needle is fine, it can be backed out of the fabric when it is necessary to remove a stitch.

Cotton-wrapped polyester thread is recommended for most beadwork projects. The cotton fibers make the thread easy to handle, and the polyester core provides added strength. The thread can be waxed by drawing it over a cake of beeswax to reduce tangling and knotting and to help the thread slide more smoothly through the fabric. Fine monofilament nylon thread can be used for beading on net.

For beading, it is necessary to have the fabric stretched tightly in either an embroidery hoop or a scroll frame, available at craft stores. This minimizes the amount of shrinkage that occurs when the fabric is beaded and prevents the fabric from becoming puckered or wavy. An embroidery hoop is used for small projects; for larger projects, such as beaded dresses, a scroll frame is used.

If an embroidery hoop is used, select a wooden hoop with a fixing screw so it can be tightened firmly. The hoop should be large enough to accommodate the entire beading design, to prevent damaging any beads. If a scroll frame is used, it should be large enough for either the length or the width of the fabric.

For each garment section to be beaded, cut a piece of fabric that is large enough to allow for any shrinkage that will occur when the fabric is beaded. When positioning the fabric in the hoop or frame, it is important that the grainlines of the fabric are squared, especially on beaded garments; if not, the garment will not hang correctly.

The pattern seamlines and cutting lines and the beadwork design are marked on the right side of the fabric. If a scroll frame is used, the fabric is marked before it is positioned in the frame; if an embroidery hoop is used, the fabric is marked after it is in the hoop. Simple beadwork designs can be marked freehand, but it is easier and more accurate to mark detailed designs using a marking tool called a *pounce pad*. The pounce pad, filled with cornstarch or charcoal, is rubbed over a perforated pattern to transfer marking dots to the fabric. A pounce pad is available from sign-painter suppliers or can be made inexpensively by filling a tennis sock with cornstarch.

An alternate method is to mark the design on a tissue paper pattern. This method is used for beading on chiffon, lace, or other sheer fabrics in a scroll frame; the tissue paper helps to stabilize the fabric during beading. The design is marked on the tissue instead of on the fabric, and the two layers are placed in the scroll frame together. The design is then beaded through both layers, and the tissue is torn away after the beading is completed.

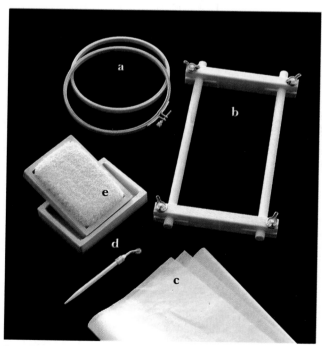

Beading supplies include wooden embroidery hoop (**a**) or scroll frame (**b**), used to stretch the fabric tightly, and tissue paper (**c**), or a needle wheel (**d**) and pounce pad (**e**), used to mark the beading design.

How to Design and Mark the Beading Design

Pounce pad method. 1) Photocopy design, or draw on paper; if beading a garment section, draw pattern seamlines, cutting lines, and grainline. Plan placement of various sizes, colors, and types of beads; plan types of stitches for sewing on beads (pages 100 and 101).

2) Pin pattern on thick layer of corrugated cardboard or cork board. Perforate paper pattern on design lines, seamlines, and cutting lines, using needle wheel.

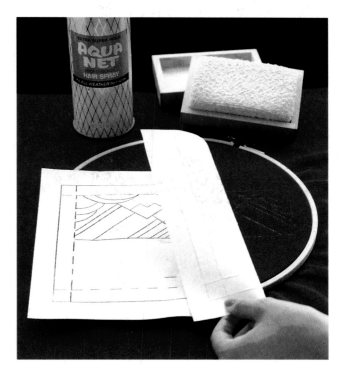

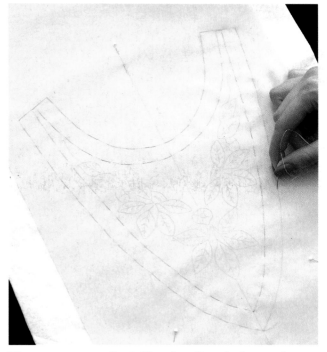

3) Place beadwork pattern, right side up, on right side of fabric; pin or baste in place, aligning grainlines. Rub pounce pad over needle holes until powder from pad sifts through holes. Remove pattern, and spray fabric with hair spray to prevent smudging.

Tissue paper method. Plan beading design, as in step 1; trace on tissue paper. Place tissue under sheer fabric, right sides up, aligning grainlines; pin. Baste fabric to tissue on seamlines and cutting lines; place in scroll frame (pages 98 and 99).

How to Position the Fabric in an Embroidery Hoop

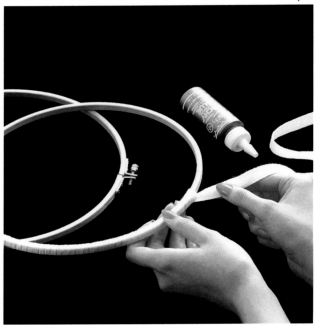

1) Secure one end of cotton twill tape to inner ring of wooden embroidery hoop, using fabric glue. Wrap ring with tape in diagonal direction, overlapping tape by half its width; pull tape firmly while wrapping. Secure other end of tape with glue. Allow glue to dry before using hoop.

2) Place fabric, right side up, over inner ring. Push outer ring over inner ring, making sure fabric is taut. Partially tighten screw and gently pull fabric until it is very taut; keep grainlines straight. Tighten fixing screw with screwdriver. Mark seamlines, cutting lines, and beadwork design on fabric (page 97).

How to Position the Fabric in a Scroll Frame

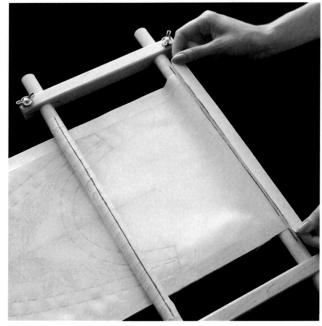

1) Mark seamlines, cutting lines, and beadwork design on fabric (page 97). Apply masking tape to lengthwise edges of fabric. Wrap masking tape around cross braces of frame. Hold cross brace firmly against table and, using pencil, draw line on cross brace where it touches table; repeat for other cross brace.

2) Assemble scroll frame. Tape one edge of fabric to cross brace, aligning the crosswise grainline of fabric to the marked line on the cross brace.

3) Roll fabric evenly around cross brace, keeping the grainline straight. If using tissue paper for marking design, roll tissue and fabric together.

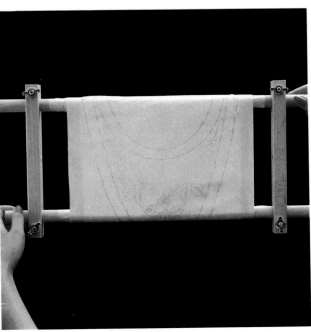

4) Tape opposite end of fabric to other cross brace, aligning crosswise grainline of fabric to marked line. Roll fabric onto cross brace to tighten fabric lengthwise, keeping grainline straight.

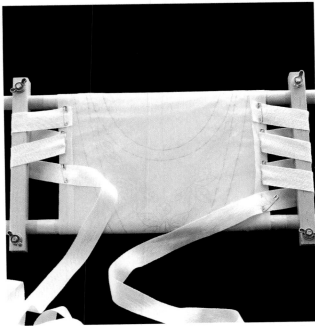

5) Pin end of 1" (2.5 cm) twill tape to edge of fabric, and loop tape over vertical brace. Pull tape slightly and pin again to edge of fabric. Repeat on opposite side of fabric, keeping grainline straight. Work back and forth across and down fabric until fabric is stretched taut.

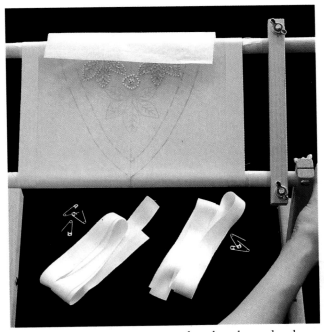

6) Place frame on supports so beadwork can be done without holding frame. After exposed fabric is beaded, unpin twill tape and place tissue paper or quilt batting over beads. Roll fabric to expose remaining unstitched area, keeping grainline straight; tissue or batting allows you to roll beaded fabric evenly, and cushions beads.

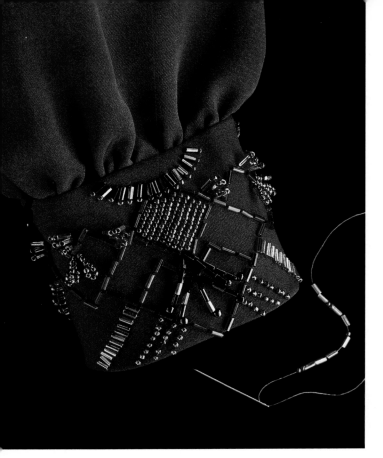

Handstitching the Beadwork

Based on two basic stitch types, the stop stitch and the running stitch, there are several variations of stitches used for beadwork. A beading needle and a double strand of waxed thread is used for beading. The eye of the needle can be backed through the fabric when it is necessary to remove a stitch. Secure the threads after every 1" to 1½" (2.5 to 3.8 cm) of stitches by knotting or backstitching.

Work from the center out toward the edges of the design. When using a scroll frame for beadwork, pass the needle from one hand above the fabric to the other hand below the fabric. To prevent distortion, do not press down on the fabric.

To make garment construction easier, stop stitching the beadwork ¼" (6 mm) from the seamlines. Compare the size of each beaded section to the pattern; if there has been shrinkage from the beadwork, adjust the cutting lines before cutting the garment section. Stitch the seams, using a zipper foot. Then complete the beadwork along the seamlines without using a hoop or frame.

How to Sew Beadwork Using the Stop Stitch

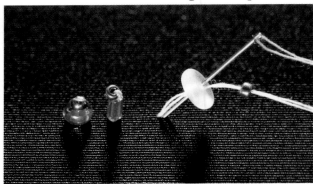

Basic stop stitch. Bring needle up through two beads on right side of fabric; the last bead threaded is called the *stop*. Bring needle back through first bead, then down through fabric to wrong side. This stitch is frequently used for attaching one large and one small seed bead, or a bugle bead and a seed bead.

Dangle stitch. Bring needle up through several beads on right side of fabric; the last bead, or the stop, is usually a small seed bead. Bring needle back through all beads except stop bead, then down through fabric to wrong side. Knot the threads on wrong side after each dangle stitch.

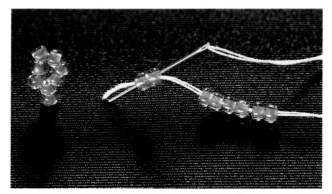

Dangle loop stitch. Bring needle up through several beads on right side of fabric; use several of these beads as the stop, forming a loop. Bring needle back through remaining bead or beads, then down through fabric.

How to Sew Beadwork Using the Running Stitch

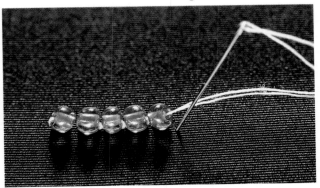

Basic running stitch. Bring needle up through a bead on right side of fabric; bring needle down to wrong side next to bead. Continue weaving needle up and down through fabric, catching a bead in each stitch. This stitch can be used for all types of beads.

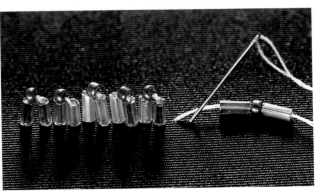

Fence stitch. Weave needle up and down through fabric, as for basic running stitch, threading needle through a bugle bead, a seed bead, and a second bugle bead in each stitch. Take a short stitch so bugle beads stand on end.

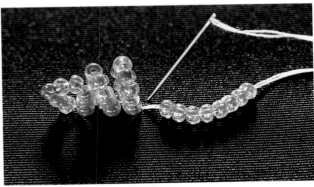

Bouclé stitch. Weave needle up and down through fabric, as for basic running stitch, threading several beads in each stitch; work stitches as close together as possible to use as filling stitches. This stitch can be used for all types of beads, but works best for round beads.

Satin stitch. Thread several beads on each running stitch, working closely spaced rows to fill in a large area. For napped fabrics, place a piece of felt, cut to shape, in the design area; this prevents beads from sinking into nap.

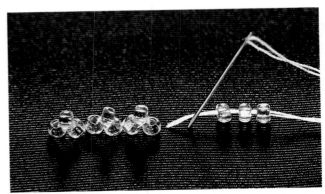

Edging stitch. Bring needle up through three beads on right side of fabric. With second bead raised away from fabric, take short stitch so third bead lies next to first bead. Take next stitch close to previous stitch. This stitch works best for round beads and is often used at edges of appliqués.

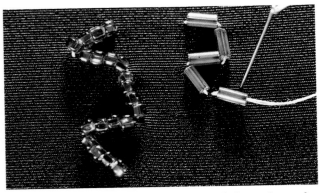

Vermicelli stitch. Weave needle up and down through fabric as for basic running stitch, threading one or more beads in each stitch; take each stitch in a different direction to form zigzag pattern.

Beaded Appliqués

For elaborate designs on large projects, such as garments, it is easier to make a beaded appliqué and attach the appliqué by hand than it is to sew the beading directly to the project. The appliqués can be easily removed before the project is dry-cleaned, to ensure that the beading will not be damaged during cleaning.

For appliqués, the beading is done through two layers of lightweight fabric, such as organza, in a color that matches the project as closely as possible.

How to Make a Beaded Appliqué

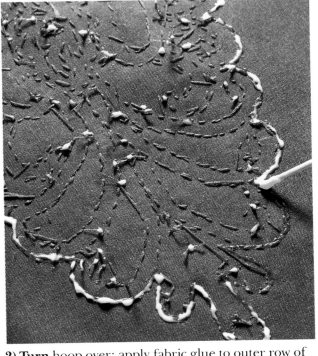

1) Position two layers of organza in embroidery hoop, and mark beading design (pages 97 and 98). Use beading design that has relatively smooth edges, avoiding jagged lines at edge of appliqué. Apply beads, using stitches on pages 100 and 101.

2) Turn hoop over; apply fabric glue to outer row of stitches on wrong side of fabric, using wooden pick. Also apply dot of glue to knotted thread ends. Allow glue to dry.

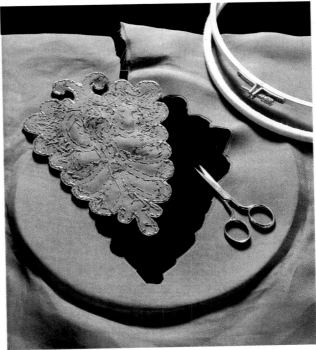

3) Remove fabric from hoop. Cut on outer edges of design, as close as possible to stitches without cutting them, using sharp embroidery or appliqué scissors.

4) Stitch appliqué to project next to outer row of beads, using basting stitches; take care that stitches are hidden between beads on right side. Baste around center area of appliqué to support the weight of the appliqué and to keep it from shifting.

Suede Lace

For a luxurious effect, synthetic or natural suede can be embellished with cutwork designs resembling the look of lace. Suede lace can be used to accent a collar or pocket, to border a suede skirt, or to embellish home decorating accessories.

The openings are cut into the suede, using an artist's knife and a few simple leather punch tools. Unlike the openings in traditional cutwork, openings in suede are not stitched, because they will will not ravel.

Select a lace to use as a guide for making the cutwork pattern. The lace design can be simplified to adapt it for cutwork openings. For accuracy in cutting, the pattern should not be reused.

YOU WILL NEED

Lace, used as guide for cutwork pattern.

Plastic tracing film with matte finish, available from leather craft stores, used for durable pattern that cuts easily.

Spray adhesive, used as temporary bond to keep pattern from shifting; spray adhesive will not harm fabric.

Cutting mat or tooling board.

Artist's knife with curved and straight blades; replacement blades.

Leather punch tools, available from leather craft supply stores.

Mallet, either wooden, rubber, or rawhide.

Cutting and punch tools include single-blade punch tools (**a**), round-hole punch tools (**b**), straight-blade artist's knife (**c**), and curved-blade artist's knife (**d**).

How to Make Suede Lace

1) Mark cutting lines of pattern on plastic tracing film. Press lace to shape of pattern piece, using steam; use seamline of pattern as guide for placement of outer edge of lace. Secure lace to pattern with removable tape.

2) Place tracing film over lace, matching cutting lines. Trace lace design on tracing film to mark the cutwork openings, adapting design lines as desired. Remove tracing film.

3) Spray reverse side of plastic tracing film with spray adhesive; keep work area covered with paper when adhesive is being sprayed and while it is wet. Place tracing film, adhesive side down, on right side of suede.

4) Cut suede and film on cutting lines. Punch out the design areas over cutting mat by pounding punch tool with mallet. Or cut on design lines, using artist's knife. Remove film from suede.

Tips for Cutting Cutwork Openings

Use curved-blade artist's knife to cut curved edges, following design traced from lace.

Use straight-blade artist's knife to cut straight edges, following design traced from lace.

Use single-blade punch tool to cut straight ends of an opening; select a blade equal in width to opening. Cut long edges of opening, using straight-blade artist's knife or single-blade punch tool.

Use round-hole punch tool to cut rounded ends of an opening. Cut long edges of opening, using straight-blade or curved-blade artist's knife.

Creative Projects
Portfolios, Bags & Belts

Portfolios

Portfolios are especially useful for business or school. A basic portfolio can be varied by adding a decorative closure, changing the shape of the flap, or making a contrasting flap.

For the body of a basic portfolio, cut one 29" × 15½" (73.5 × 39.3 cm) piece from outer fabric, interfacing, and lining. For the side panels, cut two 10½" × 2¾" (26.8 × 7 cm) pieces from outer fabric. For the inside divider, cut one 15½" × 10½" (39.3 × 26.8 cm) piece from outer fabric. For ⅜" (1 cm) binding, cut 2½" (6.5 cm) bias strips and piece them together, as necessary, for a combined length of 2¾ yd. (2.55 m).

If a contrasting flap is desired, cut the body and flap as follows. For the body, cut one 23" × 15½" (58.5 × 39.3 cm) piece from outer fabric and interfacing. For the flap, cut one 7" × 15½" (18 × 39.3 cm) piece from flap fabric and interfacing. Cut the lining, side panels, inside divider, and binding strips the same as for the basic portfolio. Apply the interfacing, and seam the body and the flap together in a ½" (1.3 cm) seam; then follow the instructions for the basic portfolio.

To make a more rigid portfolio, cover a piece of plastic canvas with fabric and insert it in the completed portfolio to use as an additional divider. Cut one 21½" × 15" (54.8 × 38 cm) piece of outer fabric and one 10¼" × 14¼" (26.2 × 36.2 cm) piece of plastic canvas.

YOU WILL NEED

Outer fabric, heavyweight and durable.

Lining fabric.

Fusible interfacing.

Button, snap, or hook and loop tape, for closure.

Plastic canvas, 10¼" × 14¼" (26.2 × 36.2 cm), for optional rigid divider.

1) Cut fabric (page 110). Apply interfacing to wrong side of outer fabric for body of portfolio. Pin lining over interfacing. Mark two foldlines, with one foldline 11½" (29.3 cm) from one short end and the second foldline 11" (28 cm) from first foldline; machine-baste on marked lines. Cut flap to desired shape.

2) Finish upper edges of portfolio and side panels; finish lower edges of side panels if fabric ravels. At upper edges, turn under ½" (1.3 cm); stitch in place.

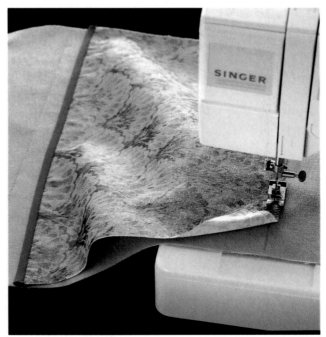

3) Stitch binding to upper long edge of inside divider, enclosing edge (page 61). Finish lower edge if fabric ravels. Place divider, right side up, over center portion of body of portfolio, with lower edge extending ¼" (6 mm) beyond bottom foldline. Stitch ¼" (6 mm) from lower edge of divider.

4) Place side panels over divider, with right sides up and raw edges even, aligning upper edge of each side panel to foldline. Baste on outer edge through all layers.

5) Apply binding, starting 12" (30.5 cm) from end of binding strip, to outer edge of portfolio, from bottom foldline on one side, around flap, to bottom foldline on other side. Stitch as for bound edge on page 61, step 1.

6) Fold portfolio on bottom foldline; press. Pin the remaining long edges of side panels to front of bag, aligning upper edges. Continue stitching binding to outer edges on front of portfolio. Cut excess binding ½" (1.3 cm) from upper edge.

7) Fold ends of binding to inside; fold binding around edges. Stitch in the ditch, as on page 61, step 2; for easier handling, stitching may stop 2" (5 cm) from bottom foldline on both sides of portfolio.

8) Stitch front and back of portfolio together for 2" (5 cm) at lower end of each side. Lightly press flap in place. Remove basting stitches at foldlines. Apply closure.

Rigid divider. Fold fabric in half crosswise, right sides together; stitch ¼" (6 mm) seams on sides. Turn right side out; press. Insert plastic canvas. Fold under ¼" (6 mm) on raw edges; slipstitch closed. Place divider in portfolio.

Jewelry bag, above, is made from screen-printed fabric.

Evening bag, below, made from twisted silk, is embellished with machine-stitched beadwork.

Zippered Bags

Zippered bags can be made in several sizes. These lightly padded bags can be used as cosmetic bags, jewelry pouches, or evening bags, depending on the fabrics and embellishments used.

For each bag, you need one rectangle each of outer fabric, polyester fleece, and lining. Cut the rectangles twice the length of the bag plus ½" (1.3 cm) by the width of the bag plus ½" (1.3 cm); this includes ¼" (6 mm) seam allowances. For example, for a finished size of 5" wide × 4" long (12.5 × 10 cm), cut 5½" × 8½" (14 × 21.8 cm) rectangles.

YOU WILL NEED

Outer fabric, polyester fleece, and lining fabric.

One zipper, at least ½" (1.3 cm) longer than cut measurement for upper side of bag.

Travel bags in various sizes and shapes are trimmed with slentre braids.

How to Sew a Basic Zippered Bag

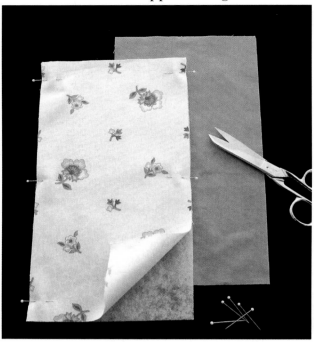

1) **Cut** one rectangle each from outer fabric, polyester fleece, and lining (page 114). Place outer fabric, right side up, on fleece; pin.

2) **Pin** a closed zipper to one upper edge of outer fabric, right sides together, aligning raw edge of fabric to edge of zipper tape; ends of zipper may extend beyond fabric. Stitch ¼" (6 mm) seam, using zipper foot.

3) **Align** opposite side of bag to zipper, right sides together, and stitch, as in step 2.

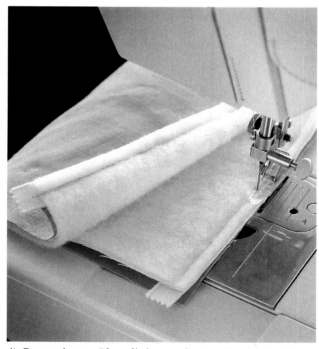

4) **Open** zipper. Place lining and outer bag right sides together, matching along one upper edge, with zipper sandwiched between layers. With fleece facing up, stitch over previous stitches. Repeat for opposite side of the lining.

5) Close zipper partially. Pin side seams, right sides together, with lining to lining and outer bag to outer bag; match the zipper seamlines, and turn zipper teeth toward the outer bag. Stitch ¼" (6 mm) seams, leaving 3" (7.5 cm) opening in lining on one side; stitch over zipper teeth. Cut off ends of zipper.

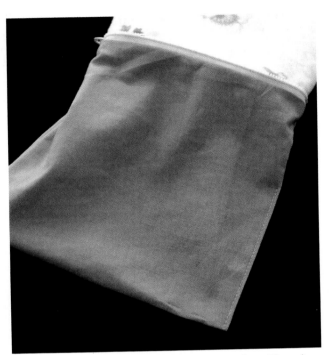

6) Turn bag right side out through opening. Turn in seam allowances at opening; topstitch closed. Fold lining inside bag.

7) Push in lower corners, from right side, to shape the box corners.

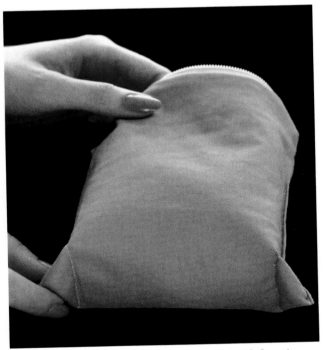

8) Turn inside out, and stitch about 1½" (3.8 cm) across corners, through both lining and outer bag. Turn bag right side out.

Shaped Belts

A basic shaped belt can be a one-of-a-kind accessory when a creative fabric or trim is used. Change the appearance of the fabric by screen printing a design, or embellish the fabric with beading or ribbonwork.

Mediumweight fabrics can be used, because the belt is stiffened by fusing a heavyweight interfacing to the fabric with fusible web. Select a fabric that will not be damaged by the fusing process, which requires steam and heat. Some lightweight synthetic leathers and suedes may be used, depending on the fabric care instructions. For the belt facing, use a durable fabric that will resist abrasion from the hook and loop tape closure.

The instructions included are for a belt with a 35" (89 cm) finished length from end to end. This size is adjustable to fit waistlines from 22" to 30" (56 to 76 cm) and includes 2" (5 cm) ease, to allow for comfort over clothing, and 3" (7.5 cm) overlap at the back. For larger sizes, additional length may be added at the ends of the belt.

This belt is designed for ⅛" (3 mm) piping. If wider piping or multiple rows of piping are used, decrease the size of the belt as on page 67, step 1.

YOU WILL NEED

⅜ yd. (0.35 m) fabric, at least 36" (91.5 cm) wide, if same fabric is used for both the belt and the belt facing; or ¼ yd. (0.25 m) fabric for belt and ¼ yd. (0.25 m) fabric for belt facing.

2⅛ yd. (1.95 m) piping to match or contrast fabric; double piping or triple piping (pages 64 to 67) may be used.

1 yd. (0.95 m) crisp nonwoven interfacing, used for crafts.

1 yd. (0.95 m) paper-backed fusible web.

7½" (19.3 cm) hook and loop tape, ¾" (2 cm) wide, for closure.

Glue stick.

Partial Pattern for Shaped Belt

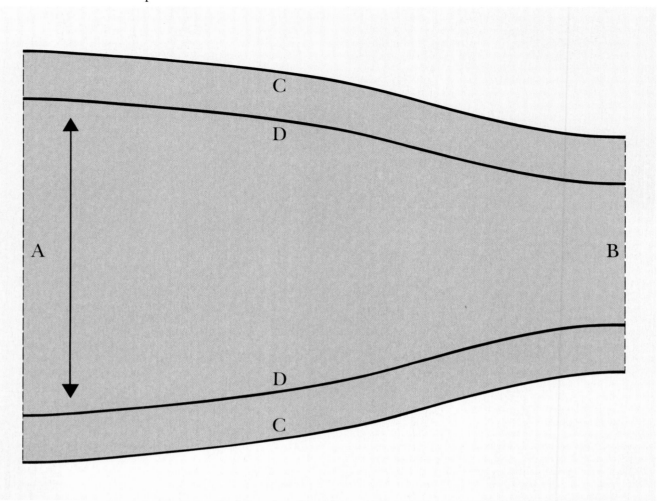

Trace partial pattern actual size onto paper, and extend Lines C and D to make pattern pieces as shown below.

How to Make the Pattern Pieces for a Shaped Belt

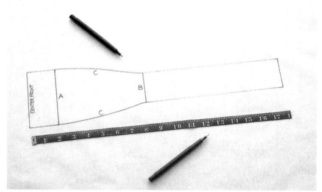

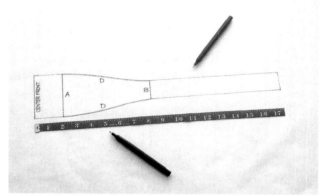

Pattern for belt and facing. Trace Lines A, B, and C from partial pattern, above, onto tracing paper. Extend Cutting Lines C, perpendicular to Line A; draw center front foldline 2" (5 cm) from, and parallel to, Line A. Extend Cutting Lines C, perpendicular to Line B; draw end of belt 18" (46 cm) from, and parallel to, center front line.

Pattern for interfacing and fusible web. Trace Lines A, B, and D from partial pattern, above, onto tracing paper. Extend Cutting Lines D, perpendicular to Line A; draw center front foldline 2" (5 cm) from, and parallel to, Line A. Extend Cutting Lines D, perpendicular to Line B; draw end of belt 17½" (44.3 cm) from, and parallel to, center front line.

How to Sew a Shaped Belt

1) Cut one belt and one facing, using pattern, opposite. Cut two pieces each of interfacing and fusible web, using pattern, opposite. Cut one belt carrier, 1⅜" × 5" (3.5 × 12.5 cm).

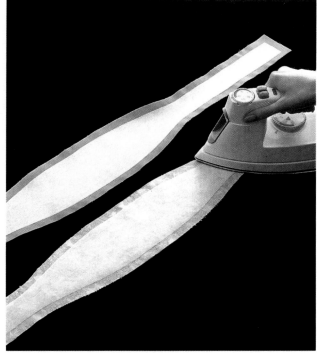

2) Apply one piece of fusible web to one piece of interfacing, according to manufacturer's directions. Fuse interfacing to wrong side of belt. Repeat for facing.

3) Fold ½" (1.3 cm) seam allowance on long edges of belt over interfacing; press. At corners, notch seam allowance and press at angle. Pink seam allowances, if desired. Repeat for facing.

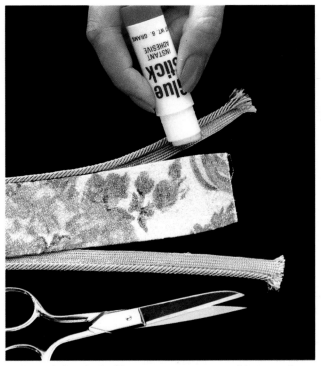

4) Cut piping in half. Baste to upper and lower edges of belt, on wrong side, using glue stick. Trim ends of piping even with raw edges.

(Continued on next page)

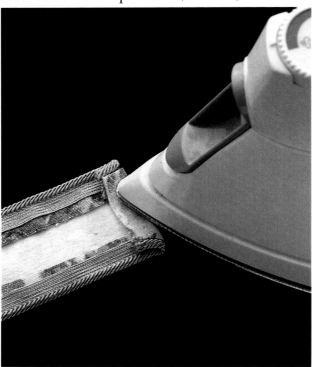

5) Fold ½" (1.3 cm) seam allowance at short ends of belt over interfacing; press. Repeat for facing.

6) Stitch loop side of hook and loop tape to belt facing, 1" (2.5 cm) from one end. Cut 1½" (3.8 cm) strip from hook side of tape; stitch to right side of belt, 1" (2.5 cm) from other end.

7) Fold ¼" (6 mm) to wrong side on long edges of belt carrier; press. Fold carrier in half lengthwise; press. Topstitch on both long edges.

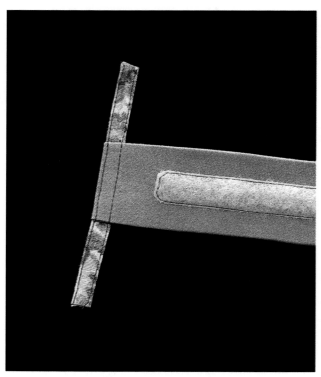

8) Center belt carrier on wrong side of belt facing, at end with loop tape; topstitch in place.

9) Align wrong side of belt facing to wrong side of belt; glue-baste in place.

10) Topstitch belt close to long edges, using zipper foot.

11) Slipstitch belt facing to belt at short ends.

12) Fold belt carrier around other end of belt; adjust length of carrier, as necessary, so end of belt slides through it easily. Handstitch ends of carrier securely.

More Creative Ideas

The various techniques shown throughout the book can be applied to portfolios, bags, belts, and other projects. Make your projects special by creating your own fabric, adding a creative detail, or embellishing it with a unique trim.

The scarf shown here was the inspiration for creating the portfolio, zippered bag, and belt. The designs in the scarf were adapted to paint the fabric for the zippered bag and for the beadwork on the belt. The unusual colors in the scarf inspired the color selections for the fabrics in the portfolio.